Masters
of cinema

ICE SKATING

LONDON ICE CLUB
...NIGHT at WESTMINSTER
...ICE CLUB
...at RICH...
...UNDERG...

791.430233092 HIT/KRO

2

Contents

Alfred Hitchcock on the set of *Frenzy* (1972).

Introduction

Who was Alfred Hitchcock? Despite four biographies, there are still many unanswered questions about the years when he was growing up over a greengrocer's shop in London's East End. Were the Hitchcocks small shopkeepers or were they the kind of people the English establishment still looked down on as being 'in trade'? Did their Roman Catholicism saddle them with minority status in Protestant England? Was Hitchcock, as Peter Viertel told me, 'a Cockney jumped up to the big time'? Perhaps only a cockney could have invented the satirical British persona that he adopted in America, where he was known as 'the Master of Suspense'.

Just how important was the fact that three of his grandparents were Irish?[1] After all, Hitchcock brought Sean O'Casey's *Juno and the Paycock* to the screen with the Abbey Players, and *Under Capricorn* (1949) is one of the few films ever made about the Irish diaspora.[2] But when I noticed a crystal shamrock on a side table in the living room of his daughter Patricia's Los Angeles home, she said she had no idea where it came from.

Was his upbringing severe? When Hitchcock was five, his father turned him over to the local constable to be locked in a cell and released after five minutes with the warning: 'This is what we do to naughty boys'. It was a ghastly thing to do to a child. Curiously, Hitchcock told François Truffaut[3] that he was a very well-behaved child — his father referred to him as 'my lamb without a spot'. But that is a biblical epithet for Christ the sacrificial victim (John 17:20, 1 Peter 1:19). He always said he wanted the constable's words inscribed on his tombstone: 'This is what we do to naughty boys.'[4]

Whatever was going on with William Hitchcock, the extended family seems to have been a jolly group, fond of picnics and other excursions. It was from his parents that Hitchcock acquired a passion for the theatre, becoming a lifelong 'first-nighter', and this paved the way for the definitive passion that was already taking hold of him when he set out at eighteen, three years after his father's death, to make his way in life.

Alfred Hitchcock on the set of *The Birds* (1963).

The Silent Period

From *The Lodger* to *Blackmail*

Alfred Hitchcock on the set of *The Pleasure Garden* (1925).

Right: young Alfred Hitchcock with his father in front of his family greengrocery store.

The greengrocer's son sets out on his travels

In 1927, six films were released by a new British director whom the critics were calling 'the young Master Mind'. Not many years before that, the young Master Mind had been working in the advertising department of Henley's, a company that made electric cables, drawing advertisements and contributing short stories to the magazine published by his fellow employees. His last contribution began with an allusion to a play the author had seen about 'a little man seeking the goal of worldly greatness' by learning to read and write.[5]

Hitchcock's passport to worldly greatness was the art classes he had taken at Goldsmiths' College, part of London University, which enabled him to move from the sales department at Henley's to the advertising department, then to writing and drawing title cards for films, and in fairly short order to designing sets. Before that, he had studied filmmaking by reading professional journals, writing scripts and hanging around the studios near London. His first job in the film industry was at Famous Players-Lasky.[6] After absorbing American production methods at that British offshoot of Paramount, he found a new home at Gainsborough Pictures, where his growing responsibilities enabled him to hire as his assistant Alma Reville, an editor and script supervisor who had lost her job when Famous Players closed in 1922. He had an ulterior motive — he was in love with her. At this point, Hitchcock was working on films directed by a flamboyant man named Graham Cutts,[7] and he became proficient at screenwriting, assistant direction and production design.

One of his last collaborations with Cutts, *The Blackguard* (1925), was a British–German co-production made at the UFA studios in Berlin.[8] There Hitchcock watched F. W. Murnau directing *The Last Laugh* (1924) and discussed filmmaking with him on the set. When he was required to order the destruction of a forest built for Fritz Lang's *The Nibelungen* (1924) in order to create a dream sequence in Heaven for *The Blackguard*, he remembered Murnau's lessons and enlarged the heavenly host by filling the back rows with midgets and dolls. As Hitchcock recalled it, the angels performed a prophetic gesture — raising their right arms in unison — when he jerked the chain linking the dolls.[9]

First Hitchcock

Hitchcock always maintained that he had never thought of becoming a director before the head of

7

Shooting of *The Pleasure Garden* (1925).

Gainsborough, Michael Balcon, asked him to direct two British–German co-productions at the MLK studios in Bavaria. The second of these, *The Mountain Eagle* (filmed in 1925, released in 1927), is lost. The first (also filmed in 1925 and released in 1927) was a risqué melodrama called *The Pleasure Garden*.

The first scene of *The Pleasure Garden* is pure Hitchcock — a dirty old man in the front row of the stalls at the eponymous theatre is caught studying the chorus girls' legs through his opera glasses by one of the girls he has focused on. This inaugural gesture of the oeuvre — which Hitchcock's cinema will never forget — is the addition of an eye to a theatrical event, which transformed it into a spectacle that is being seen from a particular point of view, thereby giving the spectator of the film the best seat in the house'. With that privileged position came certain responsibilities.

Before his first two films had even been released, Hitchcock asked Balcon to let him film an adaptation of the popular novel *The Lodger*, starring matinee idol Ivor Novello as the aristocratic title character whose landlady suspects he may be 'The Avenger' — i.e. Jack the Ripper. Hitchcock considered *The Lodger* (filmed in 1926, released in 1927) 'the first real Hitchcock film'.

In the novel a landlady, Mrs Bunting, suspects that her lodger is a serial killer, but can't go to the police because she and her husband need the money he's paying them for his room. The star system dictated a happy ending for the film, with the lodger (Novello), who has taken a room in Whitechapel to hunt for his sister's murderer, exonerated and married to the Buntings' daughter Daisy.

The film's first image, a close-up of a woman being murdered, is not followed by a reverse shot showing the murderer — only descriptions being churned through the media mill during a documentary-style prologue in which news of the latest murder spreads like wildfire. In fact, we never see the real Avenger. The Avenger is the first MacGuffin, Hitchcock's term for an empty narrative pretext (microfilms in *North by Northwest* (1959), for example), a void that nevertheless keeps everything in motion. After the Buntings are introduced, an off-screen figure throws its shadow on their door, which opens to reveal a man who exactly matches the image that has been built up in our minds

The Hitchcock cosmos

The Pleasure Garden

In the first shot of Hitchcock's first film, the camera moves along a line of men in a theatre audience. When one of them squints through his monocle, we see a blurry reverse shot of the chorus line. He switches to opera-glasses, and we share his view as he scans the legs on display, picks out one pair and focuses on the owner, who makes a face at him when she realizes she's being spied on.

Shot–reverse shot editing – showing a character, then what he sees, or vice versa – had been standard practice in cinema for more than a decade when Hitchcock made this film. The opera-glasses shot was probably inspired by a similar shot in Fritz Lang's *Mabuse the Gambler* (1922), much remarked on at the time. But in his first film Hitchcock swerves away from Lang's customary practice and begins laying down the premises of his own style, which will become the Hitchcock cosmos. The voyeur goes backstage and asks to meet the dancer he fancies, but she demolishes his attempt at courtly rhetoric – 'I've fallen in love with that delicious spit-curl of yours' – by pulling off the false curl and handing it to him. 'I'm sure you two will be very happy together', she says, leaving him holding his fetish.

Hitchcock described the origin of his cinema to Truffaut as follows: 'The idea of photographing actions and stories came about with the development of techniques proper to film. The most significant of these, you know, occurred when D. W. Griffith took the camera away from the proscenium arch, where his predecessors used to place it, and moved it as close as possible to the actors.' Re-enacted in the first images of his oeuvre, this becomes the transgression from which the Hitchcock cosmos is born, and his use of point-of-view editing will always bear its trace.

For example, the misdemeanour committed by the man with the opera glasses is immediately tarred with the brush of predatory crime when we see a purse belonging to an inexperienced country girl from the viewpoint of two thugs who proceed to pilfer the contents. Their brothers under the skin, a pair of well-dressed stage-door Johnnies, spot the same victim as likely sexual prey, until the savvy chorus girl we have just met chases them off.

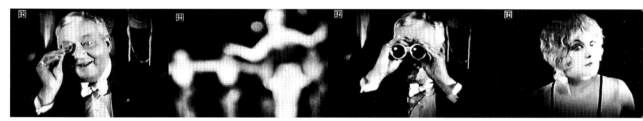

The Pleasure Garden (1925).

during the media frenzy. The way signs of his guilt pile up after that is a brilliant parody of German Expressionism, the tone being set by Novello's camp performance, which Hitchcock sends up by having a cuckoo clock announce the time, startling him as he steps through the door.

The Avenger specializes in blondes, and when the lodger sees portraits of blonde girls hanging in his room, he turns them to the wall. Later we learn that they reminded him of his murdered sister. But his nightmare won't be over when the real Avenger is caught, even though a doctor assures Daisy that he will recover — over his hospital bed hangs a painting that has been discreetly turned to the wall.

Boy wonder

During his apprenticeship Hitchcock became friends with the intellectuals of the London Film Society, which was started in 1925 to bring foreign films to London. His rise had been facilitated by the

Alfred Hitchcock on the set of *The Mountain Eagle* (1926).

fact that films were still regarded by many in the industry as an amusement for the lower classes, but when he started directing, he would need the help of his Film Society friends to fight the anti-intellectual mindset of industry stalwarts, which almost nipped his career in the bud.

When a cinema distributor named C. M. Woolf (whose mind had perhaps been poisoned by the envious Cutts) rejected *The Lodger* as too 'arty', Balcon hired Film Society member Ivor Montagu to act as consultant editor. Amazed at what he saw, Montagu recommended changes that Hitchcock readily agreed to. Once Woolf lifted his veto, the

film was released to critical acclaim and great box-office results. Hitchcock now felt financially secure enough to marry Alma.

His last two pictures at Gainsborough were *Downhill* (made in 1926, released in 1927) and *Easy Virtue* (1927), based on melodramas written for the stage by Ivor Novello and Noel Coward respectively about scapegoats: innocent protagonists who suffer for the wrongdoings of others. Hitchcock uses avant-garde visual techniques in *Downhill* to portray a young aristocrat's descent into the abyss after his father unjustly disinherits him. In *Easy Virtue* such visual experiments are largely confined to the

Hannah Jones and Isabel Jeans in *Downhill* (1927).

Opposite page: Anny Ondra in *Blackmail* (1929).

Elizabeth Allan in *The Lodger* (1926).

initial courtroom sequence: a dazzling mini-film that explores the cinematic potential of a form of theatre that Hitchcock regularly enjoyed as a spectator of trials at London's Old Bailey.

The last Hitchcock film released in 1927 was *The Ring*, his first for the company he had moved to, British International Pictures. It had been quite a year for him: the release of three films that sat on the shelf until Montagu broke the log-jam, followed by three more that secured his reputation as the best director in England. That year also marked the beginning of his love affair with the press. For the documentary-style prologue of *The Ring*, a fairground was constructed, and a newspaper article invited the public to attend: 'The film's director,

Mr. Alfred Hitchcock, will be moving among the crowds giving instructions to his cameramen (many of whom will be hidden from view) ... disguised as a showman wearing the traditional frock coat and red silk handkerchief and ebullient silk hat.' This publicity stunt could be an early statement about Hitchcock's art, which he defined as 'directing the audience'.

Hitchcock told Truffaut that *The Ring*, for which he received sole screenplay credit, was 'the second Hitchcock film'. If *The Lodger* brilliantly inaugurates the long line of thrillers that would win him renown, this sophisticated love triangle set in the milieu of professional boxing is the first masterpiece to be found along the road not

paranoia of a spoiled heiress who keeps finding herself in sexually compromising situations after her father, to teach her a lesson, pretends to have lost all his money.

Hitchcock blonde

Hitchcock's return to thrillers, *Blackmail* (1929), was a company assignment after the box-office disappointments of *Champagne* and *The Manxman* (1929). In the latter he had found a way to transcend the dry sophistication of *The Ring*, where a competent but unexciting actress, Lillian Hall-Davis, had formed the apex of the love triangle. Now, Anny Ondra, a bubbly blonde Pole who had already been acting in British silents, became a great actress in Hitchcock's hands for two films before she retired, leaving an indelible mark on his work.

In *The Manxman* she plays Kate, a barman's daughter, who promises to wait for her fisherman boyfriend Pete when he leaves to make his fortune, but then falls in love with his best friend Philip, a lawyer with a promising career. She ends up married to Pete and pregnant by Philip, who has to judge her case when she tries to kill herself.

The only flashy moment in this sober film is the dissolve from the black water that has swallowed up Kate to the ink in which Philip is dipping his pen to launch his career as a judge. More characteristic of Hitchcock films to come is a scene where we can see the filmmaker discovering what he could accomplish with this actress. Kate keeps Pete in suspense before finally promising to wait for him, changing her mind four times while the intermittent beam of the lighthouse lights up the indecision on her face.

In *Blackmail*, their second collaboration, Ondra plays a shopkeeper's daughter who dumps her boyfriend to pay a late-night visit to the studio of an artist and ends up knifing him when he tries to rape her. The wordless scene that begins when she emerges from behind the curtain where she has killed her attacker, in a state of shock, dressed in skimpy undergarments and holding the knife (see page 11), is the first in any Hitchcock film to attain the intensity of those scenes in his American films where Eros and Thanatos fuse.

taken in his oeuvre: melodrama. Critics cheered; audiences stayed away. Hitchcock would not have quite the free hand he had enjoyed for his first BIP film on the next two films: an adaptation of Eden Phillpott's stage comedy *The Farmer's Wife* and *Champagne* (1928), an original story based on a title suggested by a BIP executive and filmed, apparently, from the merest outline of a script.

Neither opportunity was wasted. *The Farmer's Wife* (1928) boasts a very funny second act where the hero engages in serial marriage proposals, disrupting a party that is already coming apart at the seams. *Champagne*, on the other hand, while officially a comedy, is really a companion piece to *Downhill*,[10] in which the camera channels the

Following pages: Betty Balfour in *Champagne* (1928).

'The Woman's Part', by Alfred Hitchcock

Hitchcock wrote this short story for the September 1919 issue of The Henley Telegraph, *an in–house publication produced by the employees of the London firm where he worked before going into the film business. It is reproduced from Patrick McGilligan's* Alfred Hitchcock: A Life in Darkness and Light *(2003).*

'Curse you!-Winnie, you devil-I'll-'

'Bah!' he shook her off, roughly, and she fell, a crumpled heap at his feet. Roy Fleming saw it all— Saw his own wife thus treated by a man who was little more than a fiend. His wife, who scarcely an hour ago had kissed him, as she lingered caressingly over the dainty cradle cot, where the centre of their universe lay sleeping. Scarcely an hour ago—and now he saw her, the prostrate object of another man's scorn; the discarded plaything of a villain's brutish passion.

She rose to her knees, and stretched her delicate white arms in passionate appeal towards the man who had spurned her.

'Arnold, don't you understand? You never really cared for her. It was a moment's fancy—a madness, and it will pass away. It is I you love.

Think of those days in Paris. Do you remember when we went away together, Arnold, you and I, and forgot everything?' [...]

The man crossed the room, and leaned upon a table, not far from where she crouched, gazing down at her with a look from which she shrank away.

'No', he said bitterly. 'I have never forgotten!'

Still kneeling, she moved nearer, and laid a trembling hand on his knee:—'Arnold, don't you understand? I must leave England at once. I must go into hiding somewhere—anywhere—a long way from here. I killed her, Arnold, for your sake. I killed her because she had taken you from me. They will call it murder. But if only you will come with me, I do not care. In a new country we will begin all over again—together, you and I.'

Roy Fleming saw and heard it all. This abandoned murderess was the woman he had sworn to love and honour until death should part them. So this was—yes, and more than that. But Roy made no movement.

Was he adamant? Had the horror of the scene stunned him? Or was it just that he realized his own impotence?

The man she called Arnold raised her suddenly, and drew her to him in a passionate embrace.

'There is something in your eyes', he said fiercely, 'that would scare off most men. It's there now, and it's one of the things that makes me want you. You are right, Winnie. I am ready. [...]'

She nestled close to him, and their lips met in a long, sobbing kiss. And still Roy Fleming gave no sign—raised no hand to defend his wife's honour—uttered no word of denunciation —sought no vengeance against the man who had stolen her affections. Was it that he did not care? No— not that, only—don't you realize? He was in the second row of the stalls!

Anny Ondra in *The Manxman* (1929).

PLEASE KEEP AWAY
FROM FRONT
of CAMERA

The English Sound Films

From *Blackmail* to *Jamaica Inn*

Alfred Hitchcock and Anny Ondra
during the shooting of the sound version
of *Blackmail* (1929).

Blackmail, second version

The sound version of *Blackmail* was made more or less simultaneously with the silent one. Ondra, who sounded like Zsa Zsa Gabor when she spoke English, lip-synched her scenes while another actress spoke her lines from behind a screen, like Debbie Reynolds in *Singin' in the Rain*. But even the silent version gives the impression of having been conceived for sound. For example, a silent scene in which just the hands of the boyfriend and the blackmailer can be seen as they haggle behind Ondra's head was reshot with sound so that their off-screen voices replace their hands, while Hitchcock focuses on Ondra's face — a displacement of attention that harks back to the voyeur with the opera-glasses picking out the legs of his favourite chorus-girl at the beginning of *The Pleasure Garden*. We are watching from the best seat in the house, but we are not in control of what we see.

    Blackmail ends with a suspenseful scene hinging on a choice between speech and silence. When Ondra starts to confess to the head of Scotland Yard, she is stopped — to our relief — by a telephone ringing, allowing her detective boyfriend to spirit her away before she can say the words that will hang her. But the last shot in

the film, of a painted jester mocking the couple as they exit Scotland Yard, reminds us that we have been rejoicing in the death of a scapegoat. The blackmailer who died in her place was guilty, but not of murder.

Theatre and its double

Hitchcock was a life-long theatregoer. The London theatre nourished his cinema from the start, and almost all of the films he made for BIP, including *Blackmail*, were adaptations of plays.

His adaptation of Sean O'Casey's *Juno and the Paycock* (1929) is filmed so that we are constantly aware that the Abbey Players are on a stage. The camera pans like a spectator shifting his attention, extending the 'best seat in the house' technique to an entire film. *Juno and the Paycock* is an experiment by a sophisticated artist who has returned to the

point he started from, after which he will systematize the discoveries he made intuitively during the silent era and create a world.

In the long jury-room sequence at the beginning of his next film, *Murder!* (1930), when eleven jurors have voted to send the defendant to the gallows, we suddenly realize we have been watching from the point of view of the unseen twelfth juror: the famous theatre director Sir John, who will eventually play detective to overturn a miscarriage of justice. The proscenium arch has vanished, but the theatrical connotations of the pointedly subjective images of jury members haranguing Sir John — an audience of one who has been following their deliberations with growing dismay — are reinforced by the film's other effects of 'theatre in cinema'. *Murder!* ends with a scene that turns out to be happening on a stage, a trick Hitchcock had already played in *Downhill* (1927).

Shooting of *The Skin Game* (1931).

Opposite page: Sara Allgood, John Laurie and
Edward Chapman in *Juno and the Paycock* (1929).

21

He next filmed *The Skin Game* (1931), John Galsworthy's play about two families battling over a piece of land. During the big auction, a long long take composed of zip pans shows the auctioneer's gaze skipping around the 'audience' from one bidder to another. The audience becomes the spectacle, holding up a mirror to the spectator in the movie theatre and, over his shoulder, to an imaginary theatre audience, whose constantly shifting attention is replicated by the auctioneer's darting gaze. On-screen audience, off-screen audience, camera and characters, are interlocking instances of 'Seer and Seen'.[11] The Hitchcock hall of mirrors

Left: *Number Seventeen* (1932).

is now in place — a cosmos of subjects that will be expanded until it encompasses the whole of the pre-Hitchcock cosmos in *The Birds* (1963).

In the hall of mirrors

In *Rich and Strange* (1932) a bored married couple on a trip around the world are split up by dalliances with strangers, then reunited after enduring a shipwreck. The film was a flop, but the first fully fledged Hitchcock thrillers grew out of this failure, which he himself cherished.

Having extended its conquest of horizontal space by sending its characters all the way to the China Seas, Hitchcock's cinema set out in the next film, an adaptation of the hit play *Number Seventeen* (1932), to conquer the vertical axis. The setting is an old dark house that is a monument to Hitchcock's obsession with stairways: three floors connected by a central staircase, with a smaller service stair behind it that is available to the characters, but not to the camera (making it impossible to understand the characters' movements at some points); skylights through which characters can crash; a cellar that doubles as a train station; and a very long flight of stone steps that lead down from there to a train.

Below: Esmond Knight and Jessie Matthews in *Waltzes From Vienna* (1933).

The multi-levelled setting symbolizes what I call the pre-Hitchcock cosmos, a cosmos of scenes where characters are defined by the place they occupy in a hierarchy — *Downhill*, for example, is full of stairways that are used to graph the hero's descent. By rendering this topography virtually unreadable,[12] the dizzying *mise-en-scène* of *Number Seventeen* completes Hitchcock's own Copernican revolution. The cosmos of scenes has been replaced by a cosmos of subjects whose position in the hierarchy depends on what they can see and how much they know at any given time.[13]

Portrait of the artist as a young parricide

Hitchcock was already plotting his getaway to Hollywood when he left BIP, but the American film industry, still reeling from the Depression, was not ready to receive him. Instead, what came next was *Waltzes from Vienna* (1933), an adaptation of a successful play about the struggle of 'Schani' (Johann Strauss Junior) to escape from the shadow of his father, Johann Senior.

Waltzes from Vienna seems to have been an especially personal film. To become famous without losing his fiancée Rasi, Johann must confront three fathers: an Oedipal one (his aristocratic patron's jealous husband, who is constantly challenging her lovers to duels in his sleep); a comical one (his future father-in-law, who forces him to become a confectioner); and an artistic one, the sadistic, castrating Johann Strauss, Sr, who keeps reminding him that, as a latecomer on the musical scene, he is only fit to play second violin in his father's orchestra. But before the concert, Schani's patron and a kindly accomplice, an older composer who may have been Strauss Sr's teacher, disarm him by setting his watch back. Tricked into arriving late at his own concert (the predecessor paradoxically transformed into a latecomer), he watches the triumph of the son whose ambitions he has always derided.

But who was the artistic predecessor Hitchcock had to overcome to achieve immortality, as he now proceeded to do?[14] On the set of *Waltzes from Vienna* Hitchcock was invited by his first patron, Michael Balcon, to join his new company, British-Gaumont, where he would work with Charles Bennett, the writer of *Blackmail*, and Ivor Montagu, who had saved *The Lodger*. This combination of collaborators was merely the situation that made Hitchcock's

Robert Donat and Lucie Mannheim in *The Thirty-Nine Steps* (1935).

metamorphosis possible. The names that shaped his inner evolution appear on a different list.

Two fathers

When filmmakers talk about their predecessors, there are influences that can be flaunted and influences that are never mentioned. Thanks to Patrick MacGilligan, we know that Hitchcock's Good Father — the one he readily acknowledged — was Cecil B. DeMille, who was his idol in the early 1920s. But when François Truffaut asked him to name a film that had made a particular

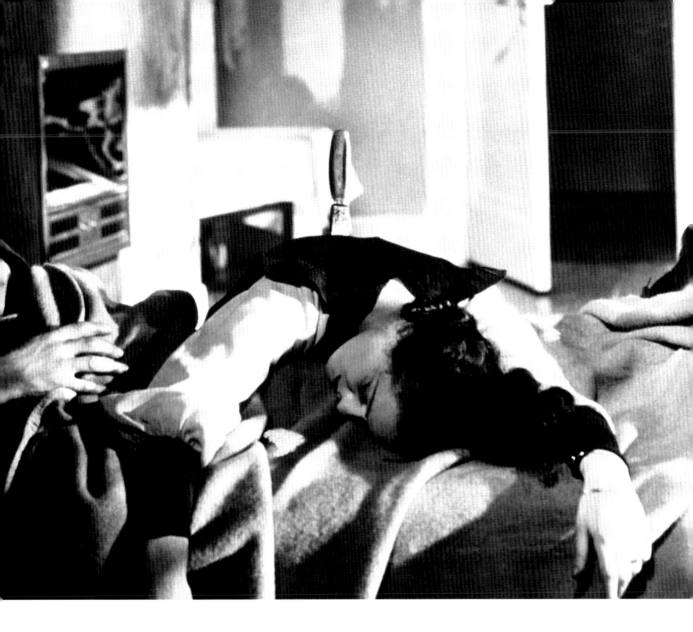

impression on him during that period he named *Der müde Tod* (1921), one of the masterpieces of German Expressionism and the first masterpiece by Hitchcock's Bad Father, Fritz Lang.[15] Speaking about *Der müde Tod*, Hitchcock identified it as 'a Decla-Bioscope picture' — Truffaut actually had to remind him of the director's name. The amnesia continued when he was asked about the casting of Peter Lorre in *The Man Who Knew Too Much*:
'Truffaut: Had you seen *M*?
Hitchcock: Yes. I don't remember it too well. Wasn't there a whistling man in it?

Truffaut: Yes — that was Peter Lorre!'
Truffaut's amazement at the memory lapse is understandable. To take just one example, the shoot-out at the end of the first *Man Who Knew Too Much* is a blatant steal from the ending of *Mabuse the Gambler* (1922). Hitchcock was not keen to acknowledge his debt to Lang because Lang's influence is so evident in his work, even before he began to make thrillers, whereas in 1962, few outside the Hitchcock circle would have thought to mention the Master of Suspense in the same breath as Cecil B. DeMille.

Cecil B. DeMille

Of all the filmmakers whose influence shaped Hitchcock's cinema, Cecil B. DeMille is the one who is least remembered today. But during Hitchcock's youth, DeMille was one of the most important filmmakers in the world.

British Famous Players-Lasky, the studio where Hitchcock got his first film job, was a British offshoot of the first Hollywood studio, later known as Paramount, which had been founded by DeMille with Jesse Lasky and Adolph Zukor. According to Patrick McGilligan, Hitchcock learned screenwriting from the women in the story department at British Famous Players, who had come from Hollywood to teach American production methods to the English. One of these was Jeanie MacPherson, who wrote or co-wrote all of DeMille's films from 1915 to 1949. Together they invented what Stanley Cavell calls 'comedies of remarriage' (*Don't Change Your Husband*, 1919; *Why Change Your Wife?*, 1920) – films in which married couples separate and reunite, which are often close to the melodramas that were already DeMille–Macpherson's stock-in-trade.

The DeMille–Macpherson comedies showcased stories about the New Woman in opulent fantasy worlds that set styles of clothing, furniture and bathroom decor for an American middle class newly liberated from Victorian mores – so much so that DeMille scholar Sumiko Higashi situates him among the creators of the Society of the Spectacle.

DeMille began by adapting plays and novels for stars from the New York theatre, and it was from London's West End that Hitchcock, at a similar turning point in the history of British cinema, took most of his subjects and actors. The adaptation of prestigious literary properties served to enhance DeMille's reputation and helped attract the middle class into cinemas.

To ratify his status as artist, he designed a medallion with his profile on it that began appearing in the opening credits of his films from 1919. The first self-drawn Hitchcock caricature profile appeared in a newspaper in 1923 – a different way of staking the same claim. Another DeMille influence: from Hitchcock's earliest days in the film business his signature – which would later be stamped on a cornucopia of merchandising spin-offs – was 'Alfred J. Hitchcock', even though few knew what the 'J.' stood for.

In the 1950s, when they both had their own production companies at Paramount, the only two directors whose names alone could sell a picture were DeMille and Hitchcock, the inventor of the 'politique des auteurs' ('auteur theory') and his most brilliant pupil. But Hitchcock's emulation of DeMille was more than strategic. On the list of favourite films that he recited for reporters when he arrived in America in 1938, those in first and fourth place were by DeMille.

Luc Moullet, the first to observe the relationship between the 'the two masters of Paramount' in his review of *North by Northwest* (*Cahiers du cinéma*, no. 102), speaks of their shared 'obsession with perfection and the box office' while noting the difference in quality: 'What is *North by Northwest* but more intelligent, more elevated, DeMille?'

According to McGilligan, DeMille's role in the anti-communist witch-hunts of the 1950s turned Hitchcock against his idol. Perhaps at that point he became a handy symbol of Cold War paranoia and of the seductive spectacle that he had created for American consumer culture to admire itself in, as if in a mirror: two illusions about which Hitchcock's post-war films were increasingly critical. But, after all, to a young man from London's East End, hadn't DeMille always symbolized not just Hollywood, where the young man dreamed of making films, but America itself?

Leslie Banks and Frank Vosper in *The Man Who Knew Too Much* (1934).

Right: Sessue Hayakawa and Fannie Ward in Cecil B. DeMille's *The Cheat* (1915).

A mixture of genres

This would not have been the case in 1932, when Hitchcock spent a year making *Rich and Strange*, a comedy of remarriage, complete with a shipwreck, that DeMille, the inventor of the genre, could have made. It was after the failure of this film, for which Hitchcock had great hopes, that British critic John Grierson reported this exchange: 'Here I should record a question asked me recently by Alfred Hitchcock: "Is cinema, then, so much a matter of violence?" For the argument in which it was put, I answered "Yes." Hitchcock went on to say that once he believed there was nothing in the novel which cinema could not do [*Rich and Strange* had been based on a novel] — the continuity of story, the description of character, the atmosphere behind, and the leisurely commentary on all three. He had come to doubt it … Hitchcock asked the question rhetorically, with the air of one who for a year or two had

been making a slow and bitter discovery … Cinema with its capacity for event should keep things happening: pulling its tension in drama from the violence (and in *complement, from the suspense* [italics mine]) of happening.'[16] After the disappointment of *Rich and Strange*, Hitchcock and Charles Bennett began plotting a story that would mix domestic comedy and espionage. BIP vetoed it, but the two men revived it when they went to work at British-Gaumont.

The Man Who Knew Too Much (1934) fused the comedy of remarriage with the sensational thriller by plunging a married couple abroad into a spy drama. The hints in the opening scenes of a romantic triangle that might threaten the marriage evaporate when the Frenchman who is flirting with the wife receives a bullet through the heart — and another kind of movie begins. *The Man Who Knew Too Much* was Hitchcock's first international hit, setting the stage for the even bigger one that followed.

Desmond Tester and John Loder in *Sabotage* (1936).

The top five Oscars for 1934 went to the first 'screwball' comedy, Frank Capra's *It Happened One Night*, about bickering mismatched lovers on the road; the film made a fortune at the box office. None of this was lost on Hitchcock. Discarding the married protagonists of his first chase film, he and his collaborators fused screwball comedy with ingredients from a spy novel by Hitchcock's childhood favourite John Buchan[17] — in *The Thirty-Nine Steps* (1935) Buchan's hero Richard Hannay (Robert Donat) spends a third of the film handcuffed to a chic sophisticate (Madeleine Carroll), who thinks he's a murderer.

Capra's film had DeMille in its DNA, but there is a more direct DeMille influence on *The Thirty-Nine Steps*, which shows the marks of *The Affairs of Anatol* (1921), a film that followed a married man with a weakness for rescuing damsels in distress through episodes with three different women. Hitchcock structured Hannay's picaresque journey around his encounters with three women, the second of whom is modelled on Anatol's second dalliance, a dour Presbyterian farmer's wife, radiantly played in Hitchcock's version by Shakespearean actress Peggy Ashcroft. Telling the story from a single point of view — the experiment first tried in *Downhill* and *Champagne* — permitted him to construct a thriller whose illogical plot twists are absorbed by a different kind of logic altogether. The expression with which Hannay greets each new absurdity he meets is the same deadpan one Hitchcock always favoured for his own performances as a raconteur. It is also the expression we wear in our dreams.

Scapegoats, Inc.

Hitchcock next made a pair of ambitious films based on Somerset Maugham's *Ashenden, the Secret*

Peter Lorre, John Gielgud and Madeleine Carroll in *Secret Agent* (1936).

Agent, which became *The Secret Agent* (1936), and Joseph Conrad's black comedy *The Secret Agent*, which became *Sabotage* (also 1936). In these films he was able to take his interest in the scapegoat theme to its logical conclusion. Innocents are sacrificed when the blundering agents in the first film kill the wrong man, and the blundering terrorist in the second accidentally blows up his young nephew, along with a bus full of Londoners.

The Secret Agent is sunk by the miscasting of John Gielgud and by Peter Lorre's on-camera dialogue improvisations, a technique Hitchcock had been experimenting with since the coming of sound. As far as *Sabotage* is concerned, the judgement of Eric Rohmer and Claude Chabrol can stand. Made with 'stunning virtuosity', it is a coldly brilliant, academic film.[18]

Whatever he said, Hitchcock must have admired Lang's *M*, because *Sabotage* closely imitates its structure. A saboteur named Verloc (Oskar Homolka) is found out first by the police and then by his wife (Sylvia Sydney), who gets to him before the official pursuers and murders him with a carving knife. There may even be a nod to Lang: the film canister containing the bomb that Verloc gives his nephew to deliver is labelled *Bartholomew the Strangler* — a home-grown version of the serial killer who is the quarry of converging manhunts in *M*.

The fact that *Sabotage* is ultimately hollow shows that even a very great artist must be careful about succumbing to outright imitation of the predecessor whose genius blocks his way. When Hitchcock said that he had made a mistake in *Sabotage* that he would never make again, he wasn't just talking about blowing up that bus.

Last English films
A charming variation on *The Thirty-Nine Steps*, *Young and Innocent* (1937) is full of ideas that will reappear in Hitchcock's American work. The most famous one comes near the end: searching for the murderer, a man with twitching eyes, the camera rises above the walls of the ballroom and descends through the crowd that is dancing to the music of a blackface jazz band, ending in a tight close-up of the drummer's eyes, which begin to twitch.

Maureen O'Hara, Leslie Banks and Marie Ney in *Jamaica Inn* (1939).

The movement recalls D. W. Griffith's dolly-in on a temple dancer on the steps of the gigantic Babylon set built for *Intolerance* (1916), but another likely inspiration is the end of the orgy sequence in DeMille's *Cleopatra* (1934): a slow pull-back along the deck of Cleopatra's ship, where dancers are showered with petals while the sails are raised and oars go into action on either side of the image, until the retreating camera reveals in the foreground the black silhouette of a drummer whose choreographed blows drive the music and direct the oarsmen.

The shot in *Young and Innocent* reverses the direction of DeMille's camera move and plants a drummer in blackface at the end of it. Hitchcock, who no doubt adored DeMille's paroxysm of Hollywood Orientalism, re-imagines it using 'American' imagery that is, in a way, just as fake: black-faced English jazzmen imitating the real thing.

The Lady Vanishes (1938), which is set on a moving train somewhere in eastern Europe, was filmed on a soundstage 30 metres long. Within this bottle Hitchcock constructed a Ship of Fools. For various selfish reasons, none of the passengers will admit to having seen Miss Froy (Dame May Whitty), a British spy who has been kidnapped by Nazi agents. The screenwriters had updated Ethel Lina White's 1936 novel with pointed anti-Nazi references — marching storm-troopers intercut with strutting geese — in the script that a second unit unwisely took with them when filming location scenes in Yugoslavia, a country that wished to maintain its neutrality. The company was expelled, the first director (Roy William Neill) moved on to another project and *The Lady Vanishes* was given to Hitchcock, who requested substantial rewrites, including the politic decision to call the enemy country Bandrika.

The heroine Iris's search for Miss Froy, the evanescent traces she finds of her existence, and the double-exposure image of her smiling face that floats between Iris and the lying faces she sees on all sides make Miss Froy a *leurre*, (a lure), a broader concept that includes MacGuffins. *The leurre*, which structures Hitchcock's narrative[19], may be a person (like the Avenger) or an object, or both, as is the case here, where a tune in Miss Froy's head is a coded message whose meaning we never learn.

She is the antithesis of her German counterpart, the master criminal in Fritz Lang's thrillers, whose hallucinatory qualities stem from his ability to cloud men's minds through hypnosis and disguise. In Hitchcock's subjective version of the Lang thriller, the *leurre* is sometimes a dead person: Rebecca, Carlotta in *Vertigo* or Mrs Bates in *Psycho*, as well as the cadavers in *Rope*, *Rear Window* and *The Trouble with Harry*, dead suns around which whole solar systems turn — hence Miss Froy's temporary transformation into a mummy. Even when she has been proven to exist, we remember the floating images of her smiling face, like a sweetly maternal ghost.

Hitchcock's last English film, *Jamaica Inn* (1939), might have continued the process by which his couple-on-the-run films had morphed into stories about a young girl's coming of age, but Charles Laughton's talkative star turn as a villainous eighteenth-century aristocrat kept getting in the way of the film that could have been. During production Hitchcock read Daphne du Maurier's next novel, *Rebecca*, in manuscript and wanted to film it, but couldn't afford to buy the rights. He ended up making it for his first American employer, David O. Selznick, the producer of *Gone with the Wind* (1939).

Young and Innocent (1937).

Opposite page: Michael Redgrave, Margaret Lockwood and Dame May Whitty in *The Lady Vanishes* (1938).

Coming to America

From *Rebecca* to *Dial M for Murder*

Joan Fontaine in *Rebecca* (1940).

Hitchcock under control

Hitchcock spent his first seven years in Hollywood as an employee of David O. Selznick. Both were admirers of DeMille, whom they sought to emulate — Hitchcock as director and Selznick as producer,[20] particularly with *Gone with the Wind*, the film he was finishing when Hitchcock arrived to start work on *Rebecca* (1940). Their relationship, as is customary in Hollywood, was a series of armed clashes, from which Hitchcock emerged victorious, at least in the six films he made on loan-out to United Artists, RKO and Fox, where he was not under Selznick's supervision.

The three films he actually made with Selznick were a different matter. On *Rebecca* Selznick not only had the final say about the script, but also edited the film and re-recorded most of the dialogue, ordered retakes and in some cases directed them himself. As a result *Rebecca* is markedly inferior to Hitchcock's English work, except for the scene where the disturbed housekeeper, Mrs Danvers (a skull-faced Judith Anderson), shows the new Mrs de Winter (Joan Fontaine) Rebecca's bedroom. Here Hitchcock achieved a terrifying fusion of sex (lesbian in this case) and death (Danvers' thinly veiled fantasy of the dead Rebecca watching her husband in bed with his new wife) that shows what the film might have been if he'd had less interference.

The adventure spectacular of the year

Rebecca won an Oscar for Selznick, but the first real Hitchcock film made in Hollywood was the first loan-out: *Foreign Correspondent* (1940), a spy thriller produced by Walter Wanger and designed by Selznick's *Gone with the Wind* production designer William Cameron Menzies. This would be a chance to make up for Selznick's decision to cancel plans for Hitchcock to direct the story of the *Titanic* — at the end of *Foreign Correspondent* he got to crash an airplane into the ocean.

Wanger allowed him to build one hundred sets, including a replica of an Amsterdam square where a diplomat is murdered in the rain, supplied with water by diverting the course of the Colorado River. Billed as 'The adventure spectacular of the year', the film was Hitchcock's bid to prove himself DeMille's equal in the domain of spectacle. He wanted Gary Cooper, who had just starred in two pictures for DeMille, as the lead, but Cooper said no. In the series of stunning scenes that begins with the assassination in the rain and ends up inside a Dutch windmill, Hitchcock and Menzies (and sound editor Frank Maher, whose creaks and moans and wind sounds contribute to the eerie ambiance inside the infernal mill) created the template for subsequent Hitchcock action scenes, like the crop-duster sequence in *North by Northwest*, which also has no musical accompaniment.[21]

Hades and Persephone

Foreign Correspondent made money, paving the way for more loan-outs, but for Hitchcock *Rebecca* would always be the film that got away. Perhaps that is why echoes of it haunted his work long after he became his own boss.

Du Maurier's gothic imagination had reactivated an archetype that had been present from the start in the English films: a young girl's coming of age that follows the outlines of the classical story of Persephone, carried off by Hades to be queen of his underworld kingdom.[22] Now Persephone and her grim consort would preside over the beginning of Hitchcock's American career.[23] The goddess makes

Cary Grant and Joan Fontaine in *Suspicion* (1941).

her first two appearances in Hitchcock's American work played by Joan Fontaine, the nameless heroine of *Rebecca*.

After making a comedy of remarriage, *Mr. and Mrs. Smith* (1941), to earn the trust of RKO, Hitchcock was reunited with Fontaine for a thriller about an innocent young heiress, Lina McLaidlaw, who suspects she has married a murderer, John Aysgarth (Cary Grant). As in *The Lodger*, the star system dictated that this should turn out to be the fruit of Lina's over-active imagination, because the public wouldn't accept Cary Grant as a killer.

Refining his earlier experiments in telling a film from one character's point of view, Hitchcock keeps the audience in doubt to the very end, when it appears that Lina's sexual awakening at her husband's hands has put her so much in his thrall that she's willing to drink the milk he brings her, which she believes is poisoned. In the shot where he mounts the stairs to her bedroom, as the moon casts a spider's web around him, he becomes

Persephone's dark husband — Death as a lover, a black silhouette carrying a glowing glass of milk to the accompaniment of a Viennese *Liebestod*, the Strauss waltz 'Vienna Blood'.

Mr Hitchcock's war

In Hitchcock's early anti-Nazi films a nameless enemy has infiltrated England — nameless because of the government's desire to preserve England's neutrality. Now Hitchcock again found himself working in a country that was attempting to stay out of the conflict.

Foreign Correspondent (1940) dramatizes the beginning of the end of American neutrality through the adventures of a naive American reporter in Europe. The film was attacked by a Senate committee that was playing to the same 3.5 million Americans who tuned in their radios every week to hear Father Coughlin, a Catholic priest, inveigh against 'the artifices of the English and the Jews' who were trying to drag America into war.

Hitchcock, of course, was English, and the producer of *Foreign Correspondent* was Jewish, as was Jack Skirball — a former rabbi who produced Hitchcock's 1942 loan-out to Universal, *Saboteur*, about the threat of American fascism. When a worker sets off in pursuit of the saboteur who has blown up a munitions plant and framed him for the crime, he discovers that the terrorist ring is run by respectable members of America's upper class.

In *Lifeboat* (1944), made on a loan-out to 20th Century Fox, a Nazi U-boat torpedoes a ship carrying supplies to England, and the survivors in the lifeboat are a microcosm of America after Pearl Harbor. When they rescue the German captain, whose submarine has sunk, he manipulates them into making him the captain of the lifeboat and steers them towards a German ship that will pick them up and send them to a concentration camp. Enraged by his treachery, they beat him to death and throw him into the sea.

The subject of these films is one that was much on Hitchcock's mind: America. Innocent like the heroines of the psychological thrillers he made during the 1940s, the nation he now called home needed to learn the painful lessons of war. The Nazis in *Foreign Correspondent* and *Lifeboat*, who have the charm of all Hitchcock villains, are the agents of her rude awakening. This was not always understood by the American press.

The U-boat captain in *Lifeboat* (Walter Slezak) is rotund, unflappable, 'continental' and sinister — not unlike Hitchcock himself, who was perceived as a threat by the defenders of America's innocence even after the country was at war. The film's portrayal of America's disarray when faced with an intelligent enemy bent on conquest, and of the savagery required to defeat him, was attacked as 'dangerous' by a few critics and by the Office of War Information, which advised Fox against releasing *Lifeboat* overseas.

The American critic Manny Farber wrote that what was theatrical about *Lifeboat* was not its single setting: 'If the events are not treated as spontaneous, unalterable happenings witnessed by an impersonal camera, but are arranged before it as though it were the eye of the audience and the events developed in order that they may be seen by the camera in the role of an audience, the process is essentially a theatrical one.'[24] In other words, every Hitchcock shot — and especially the flamboyant point-of-view shots he started using after the war — is a little theatre with an audience of one.

His favourite film

The young Hitchcock was known as the first director to put England on the screen by shooting on location. The documentary-style prologues of films like *The Ring* and *The Manxman* actually helped spawn the documentary school that would subsequently define English cinema. So it's no surprise that he tells Truffaut he disliked making films set in fancy faux English decors after coming to America: 'I wanted authentic location shots'.

Hitchcock had already begun to put his adopted country on screen in *Saboteur*, an American *Thirty-Nine Steps* which started in Los Angeles and ended atop the Statue of Liberty. Now, breaking with current studio practice, he shot as much as possible of his next film for Jack Skirball on location in the northern California town of Santa Rosa, and enlisted a Universal newsreel crew to shoot the prologue in the New Jersey neighbourhood where Uncle Charlie (Joseph Cotton), a strangler of rich widows who is sought by the police, has holed up at the beginning of the film.

When Uncle Charlie exits his rooming house, the number '13' can be seen on the door — the same number that appears on the door of the Bunting

Above: Joel McCrea
in *Foreign Correspondent* (1940).

Right: Priscilla Lane and Robert Cummings
in *Saboteur* (1942).

Following pages: William Bendix, Mary Anderson,
Hume Cronyn, Walter Slezak, Canada Lee,
John Hodiak and Tallulah Bankhead in *Lifeboat* (1944).

Alfred Hitchcock and Cary Grant

Lina McLaidlaw, the shy heiress, loves her ne'er-do-well husband John Aysgarth so much that, in the novel *Before the Fact*, she lets him murder her for her inheritance. Cary Grant would have been delighted to play a murderer, if the studio had allowed it – he had been wanting to play more serious roles – and Hitchcock saw something in Grant that made him the ideal Johnnie: alternately sinister and charming. It would be interesting to know what Woolworth heiress Barbara Hutton thought of *Suspicion* when she attended the premiere with Grant shortly before their engagement was announced.

Despite their successes, Hitchcock was unable to land Grant for *Spellbound*, *The Paradine Case*, *Rope*, *I Confess*, *The Birds* and *Torn Curtain*. On the other hand, when Grant was keen to play the wife-murderer in *Dial M for Murder*, Warner Bros. balked at his salary demands.

A decade later Hitchcock cajoled Grant out of retirement to play a cat burglar who comes out of retirement to capture a copycat burglar who has been using his methods to steal jewels on the Riviera. *To Catch a Thief* is a sunlit romp through beautiful locations, but it continues Hitchcock's exploration of his star's duality through directorial touches like the way scenes end with abrupt fades to black. These dark moments among the high jinks hint at another side to the unrepentant thief and wartime assassin John Robie, which also comes out in his barbed exchanges with the women pursuing him, played by Grace Kelly and Brigitte Auber.

The collaboration ended on a high note with *North by Northwest*. MGM paid each of them $400,000 up front and 10 per cent of the film's phenomenal gross. In one photograph of them sitting together in the hot location for the crop-duster sequence, they look like a couple of prosperous gentlemen farmers dressed for a hayride – in overalls. Richard Schickel has speculated that Hitchcock enjoyed putting Grant through the tribulations that oblige his much-married character to grow up. One particularly refined piece of sadism involved Martin Landau, who played the sinister henchman Leonard. Wanting Grant to be intimidated by Leonard, and knowing that the star had all his suits made by a certain London tailor, Hitchcock had a suit made for Landau by the same tailor, so that when he showed up wearing it for his first day of shooting, the sight would unnerve Grant.

It was while doing publicity for this film that Grant started talking to the press about his LSD therapy, and Hitchcock reportedly commented that his old friend's interest in the drug stemmed from the fact that 'LSD' in England stood for 'pounds, shillings and pence'. But *North by Northwest* would be the last trip Grant took with the Master. Perhaps after his therapy he felt no need to return to the dark places where Hitchcock alone had taken him.

residence when the suspected strangler knocks on it at the beginning of *The Lodger*. Both references hark back to *Number Thirteen*, an unfinished film about a London squat that would have been Hitchcock's first film. Having inserted this in-joke to indicate that *The Lodger* was the first real Hitchcock film, he repeats it here to announce that *Shadow of a Doubt* (1943) will be the first American Hitchcock film. It would remain his favourite of all his films.

The police are getting too close for comfort, so Uncle Charlie decides to spend some time with his sister's family in Santa Rosa, especially his niece, 'Little Charlie' (Teresa Wright). Their feelings for each other are suggested but never made explicit, just like the war that's going on outside the Edenic precincts of Santa Rosa, to which war bond posters and real servicemen in street scenes bear mute witness. Uncle Charlie reproaches himself for having brought his niece 'nightmares' in the scene where he reveals to her that the world is 'a foul sty', but he is undoubtedly Hades, come to carry her off.

In this paradise of repression, young Charlie's father and their next-door neighbour Herb stave off thoughts of the violence on a global scale that is raging unmentioned off-screen by reading mystery stories and inventing ingenious ways to murder one another. They are a potential market for the homeopathic visions of murder that Hitchcock would one day peddle on his weekly TV show, like a jolly English version of Uncle Charlie. *Shadow of a Doubt* not only put Hitchcock's America on screen for the first time; it paved the way for the invention of 'Uncle Alfred', the charming mask he would adopt in order to settle down and live there as a welcome, if slightly sinister, guest.

Alfred Hitchcock and Cary Grant on the set of *North By Northwest* (1959).

Following pages: Ingrid Bergman and Gregory Peck in *Spellbound* (1945).

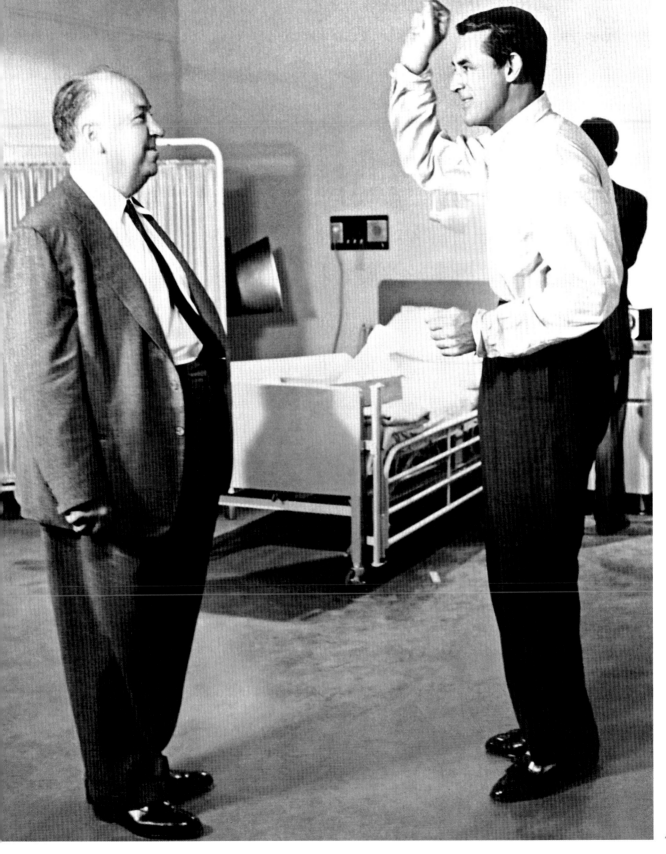

Joseph Cotten and Patricia Collinge
in *Shadow of a Doubt* (1943).

Opposite page: Cary Grant and Ingrid Bergman
in *Notorious* (1946).

The long goodbye

When Hitchcock was called back to make his second film with Selznick, the Freudian thriller *Spellbound* (1945), Selznick again edited the film himself, making drastic cuts. Despite some howlers with respect to Freud that somehow slipped past Selznick's analyst — who read the script and made her own suggestions — *Spellbound* is quite entertaining, with its bug-eyed point-of-view shots, its Salvador Dali dream sequence and Ingrid Bergman's sweet, brainy performance as a repressed psychoanalyst blossoming into new life when she falls for an amnesiac patient (Gregory Peck), who may have murdered his last shrink.

It was a huge hit — now Hitchcock was in a position to dictate his terms. During the making of *Notorious* (1946), another loan-out to RKO, Selznick, who remained the nominal producer, was barred from visiting the set or seeing rushes. But *Notorious* still has all the hallmarks of a Selznick picture: big stars (Bergman and Cary Grant), glossy production values and a darkly romantic love story.

This time the gods (the FBI) send Persephone (Ingrid Bergman) south of the equator to romance a Nazi (Claude Raines), who is building an atom bomb that could still reverse the Allied victory. Grant is the FBI agent who falls in love with her, then forces her to wed Raines. The latter is a very uxorious Hades complete with underground mineral treasures (uranium, a MacGuffin that turned

out to be real), who begins poisoning his wife when he learns she's a spy. The fact that Grant's character, before he confesses his love when he comes to save her, plays even their most intimate scenes with a stony watchful face makes her calvary all the more cruel.

The best commentary on the motives of Grant's character is the famous long take of Bergman hungrily kissing him, during which the camera becomes a third character, provoking and spying on their prolonged embrace. Male characters who send the women they love into other men's arms figure in other Hitchcock films, but in *Notorious* the off-screen triangle underlying this perverse situation — actress, actor and the director with his stony watchful face — is quite close to the surface, as it was in *The Manxman*, where Anny Ondra's potent presence elicited a similar confession from Hitchcock.

Notorious was a huge success, but Selznick showed he was the boss on their last collaboration, *The Paradine Case* (1947). He particularly disliked the long takes Hitchcock was shooting to allow the actors to perform for minutes at a time without a cut. But cinema for Hitchcock begins with theatre, and the growing importance of the long takes in the 1940s — as well as flashy devices similar to the subjective travelling shots used in John Carpenter's *Halloween* (1978) — can be understood as a return to those roots.

Leopoldine Konstantin, Ingrid Bergman and
Claude Rains in *Notorious* (1946).

Rope, an *acte gratuit*

After his contract with Selznick lapsed, Hitchcock
and an old friend, Sidney Bernstein, formed Transatlantic Pictures, with plans to produce three films:
Rope (1948), *Under Capricorn* (1949) and *I Confess* (1953).
He also signed a contract with Warner Bros, letting
him alternate films for that studio with Transatlantic
films that Warner would distribute. Transatlantic las-
ted only five years and never had a hit — it was the
films Hitchcock made for Warner Bros. that enabled
him to maintain his box-office standing. Yet the films
he did for his own company were more personal and
experimental than anything he had done before.

Patrick Hamilton's play *Rope's End* — a tale of
murder happening in real time with no act divisions
or intermission — suggested the most radical experiment: filming a play as if in a single shot. Hitchcock
described this to Peter Bogdanovich as an extension
of the 'best seat in the house' technique, borrowing

an image from the opening sequence of *The Pleasure
Garden*: 'I tried to do it as if I were giving all the
audience opera glasses to follow the action on the
stage.' But it would be more accurate to say that the
camera, as Patrick Hamilton put it, becomes 'an invisible man [who] walks about the flat [the stage] and
sees and hears everything', often wobbling visibly on
that new invention, the crab dolly, which had been
perfected for Hitchcock's *The Paradine Case* (1947).
There are many possible responses to *Rope* — different ways of being aware, or unaware, of the absence
that has been, so to speak, increasingly present in
Hitchcock's 1940s films.

In *Rope* we can watch every move of the
camera, because it is never effaced as it would be in
a normal film by cutaways to characters seeing what
the camera just saw. There is, too, a dead body in
the trunk placed at the front of the image, a threat
swelling in the off-space of the film like the figure

The emotion in the foreground
Notorious

Alicia (Ingrid Bergman) has fallen in love with her FBI spymaster, Devlin (Cary Grant), while romancing an unreconstructed Nazi who is conducting top-secret experiments in Brazil. In this sequence she reports to Devlin and his colleagues, including his boss, Prescott (Louis Calhern), who suspects there's a romance going on between Alicia and Dev. To the surprise of those present,

Alicia announces that the Nazi has proposed marriage to her. In the script the scene was described conventionally, intercutting Alicia, Dev, Prescott and the other agents as they comment on this exciting turn of affairs. But Hitchcock chose to show only close-ups of Alicia, who is devastated, and Dev, who she hopes will refuse to let her sleep with another man. As a result the scene plays as

a conversation between the two leads about this new twist in their relationship, with Dev continuing to conceal his feelings, while the other characters move around out of focus behind their backs, discussing how to take advantage of the new development. Because Prescott understands the subtext of the scene, we also get three quick shots of him looking concerned.

Having 'the best seat in the house' means seeing into the heart of an apparently anodyne scene. 'It's about the throwing away of what would seem to be the important factor', Hitchcock told Truffaut, 'putting it in the background and putting in the foreground the emotion about it.'

Louis Calhern, Ingrid Bergman and Cary Grant in *Notorious* (1946).

Alfred Hitchcock with Cary Grant and Ingrid Bergman during the shooting of *Notorious* (1946).

of *l'Absent*, the Character our mind puts in place of the camera. The other absence that structures *Rope*, constantly signalled but never mentioned, like the war in *Shadow of a Doubt*, is the two murderers' repressed homosexuality.[25] It is the motive for the murder, which is shown as a surrogate sex act, even though they think their crime is a work of art because it has no cause … like the movements of the camera. Hitchcock described the film itself to Truffaut as an *acte gratuit*: 'I undertook *Rope* as a stunt. I really don't know how I came to indulge in it.'

The figure in the carpet

Hitchcock used his hard-won freedom to deepen the moral themes of his cinema. Throughout the 1920s the young cynic had played ironic variations on the figure of the scapegoat, the innocent who bears the burden of another person's crime, in a situation where redemption through confession — the key to the 'figure in the carpet' that his French admirers would discover[26] — simply wasn't possible.

Perhaps he was trying to avoid a melodramatic device that DeMille had been exploiting shamelessly since his first film, *The Squaw Man* (1913). Even when Hitchcock uses the same device in *Downhill*, 49 the miraculous confession that exonerates the hero, who has been exiled after assuming another man's guilt (precisely the situation in *The Squaw Man*), is kept off screen. But by the time he started making thrillers in the 1930s, he had discovered a French play, *Nos deux consciences*, that would haunt him until he finally filmed it in 1952 as *I Confess*.[27] This Catholic drama about transference of guilt (to use the term invented by Claude Chabrol and Eric Rohmer) became the template for an idea that would find its fullest expression in *I Confess* and *Under Capricorn*, but its influence can already be seen in *The Thirty-Nine Steps*, where Mr Memory's unmotivated public confession miraculously pops out and links up with the 'wrong man' plot in a pattern that makes symbolic sense, even though from a realistic standpoint it makes no sense at all.

Confession scenes are hard to pull off in the best of circumstances without provoking yawns or sniggers, as Hitchcock discovered when some members of a preview audience giggled at his first ending for *Suspicion* (a lengthy confession by Johnny that he was planning to kill himself). Psychoanalysis, not religion, came to the rescue in *Spellbound*, where Peck's amnesiac feels guilty for a murder he didn't commit because he has repressed a traumatic childhood memory. Recovering it (while skiing, unfortunately) frees him … to marry his analyst. After being explored in two very personal films, the drama of guilt and confession would lend a gravitas to even the lightest entertainments Hitchcock made in the 1950s.

'The Cecil B. DeMille of decoupage'

Hitchcock finally started negotiating to purchase the rights to *Nos deux consciences* in 1946, and it took him six years, twelve writers and as many endings to get a satisfactory screenplay out of Paul Bourdes' play. As a result, the central situation — transference of guilt in the context of the Roman Catholic confessional — influenced even films that were made before *I Confess*, particularly *Under Capricorn* (1949), a film composed of breathtaking long takes that confirmed André Bazin's epithet for Hitchcock: 'The Cecil B. DeMille of decoupage'.[28]

In the novel Hattie Flusky's confession that she, not her husband, shot her brother (precisely the situation in DeMille's most famous film, *The Cheat*

Farley Granger, James Stewart and John Dall in *Rope* (1948).

Alfred Hitchcock by Peggy Robertson

Peggy Robertson was Hitchcock's assistant on the films he made after The Birds (1963). *She first worked with him in England as script supervisor on* Under Capricorn (1949) *and* Stage Fright (1949), *rejoining him in that capacity at Paramount for* Vertigo (1957). *These recollections are taken from an oral history recorded by Barbara Hall of the Herrick Library of the Academy of Motion Picture Arts and Sciences, and are used with her permission.*

A painter in the travelling shot
Under Capricorn (a film composed of very long takes requiring elaborate choreography of actors, furniture and camera) … We were just starting to dub and a young voice pipes up: 'What's that man doing there?' … It's the assistant to the assistant to the assistant of the sound editor, a boy of about seventeen. And there, as the camera moves from the kitchen into the dining room, a man has been caught by the camera. He has enough sense to remain perfectly still, and he's wearing a white jacket that a painter wears … So I was elected to go and tell Hitch … He said, 'What's the trouble?' I said, 'Well, there's a man, a painter, in the travelling shot.' He said, 'Don't be ridiculous.' … So he gets up and he comes down, and he turns at the end and says, 'Well, if people are paying proper attention to the story, they won't be looking for a man in a white jacket … Leave it. No one's going to notice.' And no one ever noticed. He's still in the picture, and you can see him.

Vermeer and Rembrandt
[After Robert Burks's departure, Hitchcock worked with a series of new cameramen.] Before we actually started shooting and the cameraman was cast, Hitch would come up to me and say, 'Buy the latest book on Vermeer …' And I had a second choice – it was Rembrandt. 'And leave it on the desk on the set … If you put it unobtrusively on the desk, when the cameraman comes around to talk, he'll notice and he'll pick it up. And maybe we'll get a Vermeer, maybe we'll get a Rembrandt … ' I mean, [if he just showed him the book and said, 'This is the kind of effect I would like to get'] the man might argue and say, 'Why Vermeer? Why don't we have Van Gogh or Rubens?' That's how he got what he wanted – not that we ever had a Rembrandt or a Vermeer. (laughs) We tried!

That cat is going to be killed!
[In the afternoon when there was nothing to do Robertson would select a new film and screen it for Hitchcock in his private projection room at Universal.] There was one film, it was an English film, and he said, 'Well, what are we looking at today?' And I said, 'You won't know anyone in it, but it's called …' So he sat down and we started looking at it. And suddenly during it … It was rather dull, and it was so comfortable in the projection room, there were big leather armchairs, and to sit back was so nice. And he said, 'What's that?' So I opened my eyes and said, 'What?' He said, 'That cat! That cat's going to get killed!' I said, 'No, Hitch, how can you say that?' He said, 'I tell you, that cat's going to get killed.' He was a great animal lover, and I wouldn't show him anything … So the moment came, and I knew it was drawing near, and that that cat was going to get killed. (laughs) It was obvious now. Even to me. And then the cat was killed. And he said, 'Cut it' to the projectionist. Didn't even wait for me to cut it. He said, 'I told you that cat was going to be killed!' I said, 'I'm sorry, Hitch, I hadn't seen the film …' He said, 'I don't want to hear any excuses' and walked out of the projection room, went in the other room, and I didn't see him for the rest of the day.

Alfred Hitchcock in *Under Capricorn* (1949).

(1915), which ends with a courtroom scene, where a wife confesses in order to save her husband,[29] comes one-third of the way through the book and is given no dramatic weight at all, but Hitchcock makes it the climax of the film — an incandescent long take around Ingrid Bergman that lasts nine and a half minutes.[30] Hattie is another Persephone, but her resurrection in *Under Capricorn*, like Bergman's in *Notorious*, is surrounded by Christian symbolism. Hitchcock would not have been unaware, for example, that the Aborigine name of Hattie's house, 'Minyago Nugilla' ('Why weepest thou?'), recalls Jesus' first words to Mary Magdalene when he finds her weeping beside the empty tomb.

The only possible ending

Under Capricorn was the biggest flop of Hitchcock's career, so he now made two pictures for Warner Bros. — *Stage Fright* (1949), a 'wrong-man' thriller filmed in England, and *Strangers on a Train* (1951), based on Patricia Highsmith's psychological thriller about two strangers who meet on a train and 'swap' murders — the psychopath Bruno murders the ex-wife of Guy Haines, who is finally blackmailed into murdering Bruno's father.

Hitchcock fell in love with the cinematic possibilities for punning visually on this criss-crossing relationship between doubles, which had inspired so many of the structural beauties in *Shadow of a Doubt*. Perhaps, if *Rope* had done better, Hitchcock would have been tempted by Highsmith's magnificent ending. Racked with guilt, Guy finally finds someone to confess to — his murdered ex-wife's lover, who couldn't care less. 'Take me' are his last words, spoken to the detective who has been listening to his confession on an open phone line.

In the film, Guy (Farley Granger), who hasn't killed anyone, is suspected by the police but finally exonerated at the carnival that was the setting for the earlier scene where Bruno (Robert Walker) stalks and strangles a woman he has never seen before. After a fight on a merry-go-round that crashes, the dying Bruno is identified by a witness and further incriminates himself by telling an unnecessary lie to the police. The dazzling editing of the sequence gave the audience its money's worth without letting them dwell on Bruno's motivations, and *Strangers on a Train* was a hit. At last, in *I Confess* (1953), Hitchcock could film the story that had haunted him for so long

— a priest hears a murder's confession and is suspected of being the murderer himself. The film was made despite the doubts of his partner, who ended up letting Warner Bros. take it on, and of the studio, which denied him two fond wishes: the hero could not father an illegitimate child before taking his vows, and he couldn't be executed at the end.

What survived were two ideas from the play: the transference of guilt and the contrast between the 'two consciences' of the play's title. The author of *Nos deux consciences*, Paul Bourde, had drawn a contrast between the village priest who hears a murderer's confession and his best friend, a socialist politician whose wife was being blackmailed by the murdered man over a love affair she had with the priest before he took orders. When the priest is accused of the crime and the politician learns of his wife's past affair, he is faced with a dilemma. If she tells the magistrate that she saw the priest to ask for his help on the night of the murder, her husband will be dragged into a scandal and lose a tight election. But when he nobly sends his wife to alibi his friend, he merely supplies the police with the missing motive. The priest is executed and, by dying, saves the murderer's soul.

Hitchcock kept the twist but changed its meaning.[31] In the film it is the politician's wife (Anne Baxter) who goes to the police to alibi Father Michael Logan (Montgomery Clift) because she still loves him … with the same disastrous results. The contrast between sacred and profane love seems to have pleased the Canadian bishop who approved the version of the script in which Logan still had an illegitimate child and was going to be executed at the end. The prelate exclaimed to Sidney Bernstein: *'Ça, c'est du cinéma!'*

Building on his experience shooting *Stage Fright* in London locations, Hitchcock shot *I Confess* on location in Montreal, taking advantage of its many churches. The struggle to find an ending for *Strangers on a Train* may have helped him finally find the ending for *I Confess*, just before the start of production. The murderer shoots his wife to keep her from confessing his guilt and is gunned down by the police, setting the stage for what seems in retrospect to have been the only possible ending: his dying confession and Logan's intoned absolution. Simple, unexpected and breathtakingly right.

Marlene Dietrich and Richard Todd in *Stage Fright* (1949).

Theatre, film and television

The three 'run-for-cover' films Hitchcock did for Warners map the main coordinates of his career, looking backwards as well as forwards into the 1950s: theatre (*Stage Fright*), film (*Strangers on a Train*) and television (*Dial M for Murder*).

1. A theatre curtain rises at the beginning of *Stage Fright* to show a high-angle view of London. As in *Murder!* theatrical devices (long takes, very noticeable point-of-view shots) co-exist with scenes of theatre-in-cinema and characters role-playing in real life — Marlene Dietrich, in particular, plays all her scenes to the camera.

2. *Strangers on a Train* begins with a metaphor for cinema much favoured by Hitchcock (and DeMille), a moving train, and ends with one that would be popular with Hitchcock's followers in the 1970s and 1980s, an amusement park ride.

3. *Dial M for Murder* (1954), which substitutes an invisible system of editing for the long camera moves of *Rope*, is the final product of over three decades of experiments with filmed theatre, but it started

life as a British television play. ('Filmed theatre' and television were often indistinguishable during this period.) The result is 'a film tailor-made for the small screen' according to Louis Skorecki, for whom it looks forward to Hitchcock's invention of 'post-cinema' in the 1950s, the period when 'he decides to sell himself bag and baggage to the small screen'.[32] But *Dial M for Murder* is also a masterful *leçon de cinéma*, whether one is getting caught up for the nth time in a 20-minute dialogue scene where a weak man is being ensnared in a clever murderer's web, or the bungled murder, where editing, colour, lighting, music and *mise-en-scène* combine in an explosion of pure cinema.

Although Hitchcock was responding with 3D to the threat of television in *Dial M for Murder*, the form it took was an hallucinatory return of theatrical space. The effect of 3D is really used only once, when Grace Kelly's arm reaches out of the screen, finds a pair of scissors and sinks them in the back of the man who is strangling her. This is Hitchcock's third colour film, and in this sequence he finally finds the colours with which to film sex and death conjoined.

Farley Granger and Robert Walker in *Strangers on a Train* (1951).

Opposite page: Brian Aherne and Montgomery Clift in *I Confess* (1953).

Master of Suspense

From *Rear Window* to *Family Plot*

Alfred Hitchcock with James Stewart on the set of *Rear Window* (1954).

Right: James Stewart in *Rear Window* (1954).

Rear Window

The run-for-cover films at Warner Bros. gave Hitchcock four moneymakers in a row (ironically, *I Confess* was profitable too) and the clout to land a deal as a producer—director at Paramount, the long-time home of Cecil B. DeMille, where he proceeded to make a series of international hits. Was he recalling the drubbing *Under Capricorn* had received when he told Truffaut, years later, that he made the kind of films he did because he couldn't rely on the critics?

Rear Window (1954), like *Lifeboat*, *Rope* and *Dial M for Murder*, is a single-set film, although the set encompasses the apartment of the main character as well as the apartments across the courtyard. L. B. Jeffries (Jimmy Stewart), a photojournalist confined to home with a broken leg, observes his neighbours, and begins to suspect that one of them, Lars Thorwald (Raymond Burr), has murdered his wife. 'Lighting this composite set was the biggest electrical job ever undertaken on the lot by Paramount — not excepting even Cecil B. DeMille's big spectacle sets', Robert Burks, Hitchcock's cameraman since *Strangers on a Train*, told the press. Hollywood was embracing the epic cinema pioneered by DeMille as a response to the negative impact of TV, but in *Rear Window* Hitchcock proposed an alternative — through a technique as novel as 3D, the one-set film becomes a spectacle.

Rear Window lends itself to so many interpretations (Plato's Cave, a movie theatre, a screen on which the unconscious is projected, a film and its maker, an ironic fable about God and his creatures) that we forget what it offered a 1954 audience. Lured by the promise of being able to spy on the neighbours, moviegoers discovered everyday reality transformed into 'The Greatest Show on Earth' (the title of DeMille's last blockbuster). Burks and Hitchcock evoke the colours of passing time during a hot New York summer, and Harry Lindgren's sound design (undiluted by underscoring) adds a sensory layer that possesses a hallucinatory reality the image alone could not offer.

Rear Window proves that movies are still the best entertainment — Jeffries doesn't even own a TV. But Hitchcock hired former radio writer John Michael Hayes to write the dialogue, and what Hayes produced was a risqué version of TV comedy dialogue: just what Hitchcock needed, since sitcoms were already seting a new standard for what was funny.

The film begins where Hitchcock's cinema begins: a man using binoculars to bring a lasci-

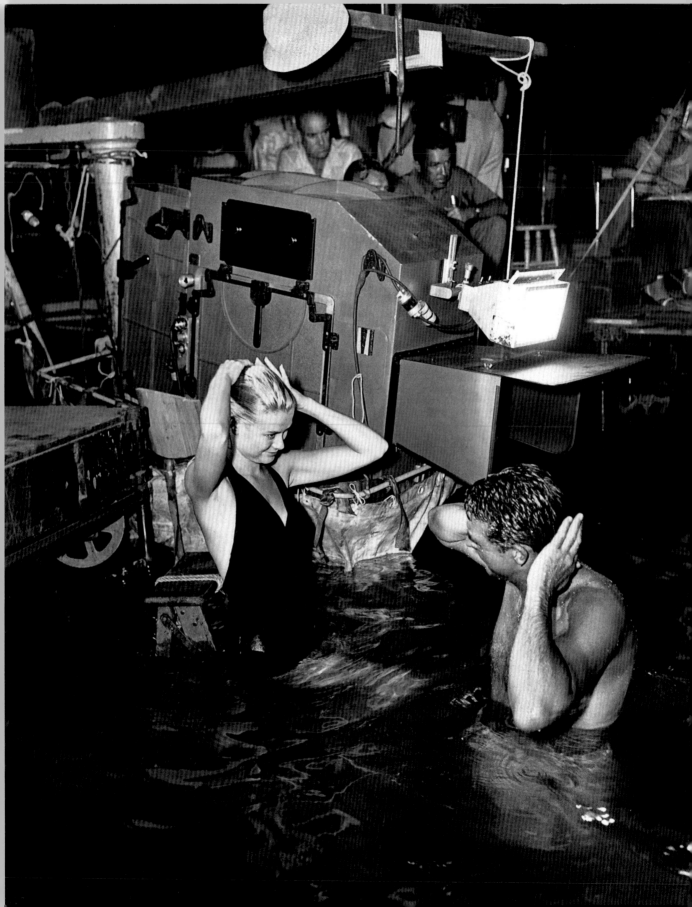

Grace Kelly and Cary Grant on the set of *To Catch a Thief* (1954).

Right: John Williams, Grace Kelly and René Blancard in *To Catch a Thief* (1954).

vious spectacle nearer. Later, Jeffries sends his girlfriend Lisa (Grace Kelly) to dig in the garden of the courtyard. Finding nothing, she climbs into the murderer's apartment, where she is caught by him and manhandled while Jeffries watches helplessly, waiting for the police to arrive. After the police take Lisa away and he is alone, Thorwald pays him a visit.

Jeffries is almost punished like the original Peeping Tom, whose eyes were put out, as we're reminded by his talkative nurse. This has been interpreted as a judgement on scopophilia, urban alienation and male chauvinism, among other things. Perhaps it is a creation myth: in orthodox Christianity the Fall comes after Genesis, but the Genesis of Hitchcock's cosmos occurs simultaneously with the Fall.[33] The fall into Original Sin in *Rear Window* (recalling Griffith's, when he passed through the proscenium arch of primitive cinema) is the moment when the cosmos of seeing subjects, of which *Rear Window* is a microcosm, was born.

Two films in VistaVision

John Michael Hayes now wrote two comedies for Hitchcock, both based on novels: *To Catch a Thief* (1954) and *The Trouble with Harry* (1956). They were filmed back to back in 1954, on the Riviera in the spring and in Vermont in the fall, showing off two very different landscapes in Paramount's new VistaVision process.

Nice and its environs are filmed in extended long shots in *Thief*, sometimes taken from a helicopter, a novelty at the time. Scenes between Cary Grant and Grace Kelly are helped by Hayes's talent for double entendres, which Hitchcock visually echoes in a famous scene intercut with fireworks

— one of several superb sequences filmed in the false night of Paramount's soundstages.

To lure viewers away from the little screen, Hitchcock offers stars trading sophisticated dialogue on the Riviera (advertised in travel brochures under the credits), even though Kelly and Grant are filmed more often than not like Lucille Ball and Desi Arnez, whose show Hayes had written in his radio days.

By the mid-1950s Hitchcock was growing more preoccupied with sex and death and more indirect in portraying them — in *Thief* they have passed into the nightshade green of the night scenes in which Grant pursues his own shadow. A retired, gentlemanly Hades who only cedes to Kelly after a struggle, he is understandably alarmed to learn at the end that 'Mother' (Demeter) will be coming to stay with them. Theoretically, that should usher in a new Golden Age, which is portrayed in Hitchcock's second VistaVision film.

The base metal of TV dramaturgy is transformed into gold in Hitchcock's early experiments with VistaVision by being associated with cinema images — in *Harry*, VistaVision paintings of a glorious Vermont autumn. But the first act of *Harry* is unabashed filmed theatre, set in a forest glade straight out of Shakespeare through which all manner of characters traipse, taking turns discovering the dead body mentioned in the title and coming to their own conclusions about it.

'Next thing you know they'll be televising the whole thing!' grumbles the Captain (Edmund Gwenn) as he watches from behind a rock — a shameless acknowledgement of how most of the film is being shot. Gwenn's genteel cockney Ubu Roi sets the tone for a film that is the restrained British equivalent of a barbaric yawp.

'Alfred Hitchcock Presents' opening credits.

Grace Kelly in *To Catch a Thief* (1954).

The spectacle of Nature's decay is beautiful, especially during the night sequence, situated at the intersection of 'Enchanted' and 'Sinister', when the weary gravediggers are returning home after burying Harry for the third time. We are in Arcadia, and so is Death (Harry), but devotees of the film have to refer to John Trevor North's novel to learn the grim reason for the title character's demise. Harry's wife (Shirley MacLaine) fled their honeymoon suite because he wanted her to imagine when they made love that he was her dead first husband, whose picture he had hung over their bed. When he tracks her down in Vermont to claim his marital rights, she thumps him with a milk bottle, starting the chain of events that turn him into the corpse he had fantasized becoming in her arms. But Hitchcock and Hayes substituted a euphemism for this unsavoury backstory at the eleventh hour, eliminating a 'terrible truth' that still casts odd shadows on Eden from just offstage.

Hitchcock and television

DeMille's appearances on the weekly radio programme *The Lux Radio Theatre* had made him a household name, so Hitchcock's first American agent, Myron Selznick, suggested that he 'do a DeMille' by producing his own programme. Selznick's brother David and Jack Warner both refused to allow it, but when Hitchcock moved to Paramount in the 1950s, he created *Alfred Hitchcock Presents* — a weekly series of televised 'tales of suspense and mystery', as he explains in his introduction to the first episode aired, echoing the title of the story collection that made Poe immortal.

The deal for the series was struck by Hitchcock's new agent, Lew Wasserman, who had

previously guided him to Paramount. The show was broadcast on Sunday nights following *The GE Theatre*, a programme introduced by another Wasserman client, Ronald Reagan, whom the powerful agent was grooming for a political career. This was television's golden age, and Hitchcock certainly contributed to making it that, while hauling off many bags of that gold.[34]

Starting with *The Lodger*, he had occasionally been obliged to change the ending of a film to please the studio or evade the censor. But the TV format permitted him to have it both ways: characters who committed perfect murders would face retribution in his final monologue, which always took a poke at the ultimate censor, the sponsor (a laxative manufacturer). These epilogues ritually act out an ambivalence that underlies Hitchcock's cinema, symbolized by the eternal couple of Persephone and Hades, Eros and Thanatos. That fusion of opposites, which is kept discreetly offstage in *Harry*, is treated almost romantically in the telefilm *The Crystal Trench* (1959), where a woman whose husband has been killed in a climbing accident spends the rest of her life waiting for his body to emerge, perfectly preserved and still youthful, from a slow-moving glacier.

Suspense is her salvation

Stating what is now a minority view of the 1956 remake of *The Man Who Knew Too Much*, British critic Raymond Durgnat wrote that the 1934 classic had been 'boringly and painstakingly reworked for the family market', with dollops of 'vicarious tourism' added — VistaVision images of Marrakesh and London, now flawlessly integrated with scenes shot on soundstages, which employ the resources of montage that were often abandoned in *Thief*

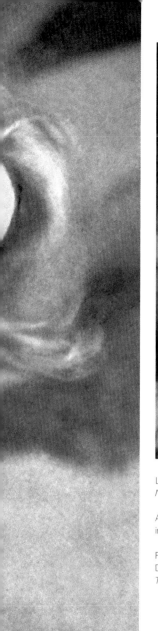

Left: Cary Grant and Eva Marie Saint in
North By Northwest (1959).

Above: Grace Kelly and James Stewart
in *Rear Window* (1954).

Following pages: Alfred Hitchcock with
Doris Day and James Stewart on the set of
The Man Who Knew Too Much (1956).

and *Harry*. In other words, the second *Man Who Knew Too Much* continues the incorporation of TV by Hitchcock's cinema. The English sophisticates of 1934 have become an American couple abroad played by James Stewart and Doris Day. With their little boy Hank, Ben and Jo McKenna are a TV family plunged into deep waters. And as on TV, while Father knows best, Mother knows better.

Every great filmmaker who enjoys a long career will eventually theorize what he has been doing intuitively all along in order to do it perfectly in the future. For Hitchcock that happened in the 1950s. The second *Man Who Knew Too Much* is better, he once said, because in the meantime he had 'learned to think of the audience'. Jean Douchet explains: 'We begin with the spectator, who has the motivations. We project them onto figures, props, relays that we'll call characters ... These characters are products of the collective mentality. They were fabricated by the media and turned into trademarks.'[35] Douchet's assertion that 'the filmmaker has turned over the *mise en scène*' to the spectator is just a striking way of saying that

Doris Day in *The Man Who Knew Too Much* (1956).

Right: Alfred Hitchcock with Henry Fonda and
James Stewart in 1957.

henceforth the spectator's projected desires and
fears will be the film. *Rear Window*, where each
member of the audience is formally installed in
the director's chair, is a film about voyeurism,
while *The Man Who Knew Too Much* is a film about
suspense, building up to the virtuoso sequence
where Jo becomes the privileged spectator of a
concert in the Albert Hall that is going to end with
an assassination.

 Whereas the heroine of the 1934 film decides after an inner struggle to risk her kidnapped
child's life by screaming when she sees the assassin about to fire, Jo screams after a whole series of
experiences, which we have shared, have reduced
her to hysterics.[36] Suspense, Chabrol and Rohmer
argue, is her salvation.[37] Hitchcock even planned
for Jo to scream when the cymbals crash, then decided that was too mechanical a solution.[38]

Reggie Nalder in *The Man Who Knew Too Much* (1956).

Doris Day and James Stewart in *The Man Who Knew Too Much* (1956).

A miracle

At the end of his chapter on *The Man Who Knew Too Much* Durgnat concludes that Hitchcock sold out at Paramount: 'Hence the peculiar dichotomy of this intimate VistaVision drama, as of a Simenon working to the functional requirements of Cecil B. DeMille.' Substituting Fritz Lang for Georges Simenon — Durgnat's example of middle-brow entertainment that succeeds as art — offers a good description of Hitchcock's next film: the true story of Manny Balestrero, a New Yorker whose life was destroyed when he was wrongly identified as a hold-up man.

TV dramas in the neo-realist vein were an influence on *The Wrong Man* (1956), a story that had been dramatized already on NBC. But Hitchcock's intensely subjective *mise en scène* and Robert Burks's extraordinary black-and-white photography, using new lighting equipment that permitted filming in the actual locations where events had occurred, lift it to a level of artistry that invites comparisons with the films of Carl Theodor Dreyer and Robert Bresson.

Hitchcock told playwright Maxwell Anderson that he wanted to make this a study of a couple under pressure as in *The Man Who Knew Too Much* — Balestrero's wife Rose had gone mad during their ordeal. There were other precedents in Hitchcock's cinema: the agonizing sequences of Manny's arrest and incarceration recall the documentary-style prologue to *Blackmail*. And Hitchcock knew the tradition at Warner Bros. of social films based on true

stories. The only sound film on his 1938 'ten best' list was *I Am a Fugitive from a Chain Gang*, a radical indictment of Southern justice filmed from the point of view of a wrongly accused man.

Lang had made two films about unjustly accused men when he first came to Hollywood; the most uncompromising one starred Henry Fonda, whom Hitchcock now cast as Manny Balestrero. In *You Only Live Once* (1937) Fonda plays a reformed convict who is going to be executed for a bank robbery and murder he didn't commit. When he escapes, a priest brings him word that the real criminal has been found, and Fonda, unable to believe this news after the injustices he has suffered, shoots him.

Lang was a Catholic, but his version of Christ — the messenger of forgiveness murdered by humanity — is grimly ironic. Fonda's salvation, announced by the voice of the dead priest on the soundtrack, will not be in this world. Hitchcock's reply to this was to film a miracle, the only invented episode in *The Wrong Man*: at his mother's insistence, Manny prays to a framed image of Christ. Intercut with close-ups of Manny's face is the figure of the real hold-up man, who emerges from the shadows and advances towards the camera until their faces merge. In the next scene the double is arrested while committing a robbery.

DeMille's pioneering prison drama, *The Godless Girl* (1929), had also ended with a miracle, but Manny's miracle comes with an ironic catch.[39] The news that he has been cleared doesn't cure

Kim Novak and James Stewart
in *Vertigo* (1957).

Opposite page: Hitchcock with Vera Miles
on the set of *The Wrong Man* (1956).

Rose's madness, and the strange last shot that Hitchcock added when he got word that Rose had finally recovered her sanity — two distant figures that are supposed to be the Balestreros living happily in Florida — is no more reassuring than the 'happy ending' of *You Only Live Once*.

The anxiety of influence

Based on a novel by Pierre Boileau and Thomas Narcejac, *Vertigo* (1957) is a Symbolist masterpiece, and like the poetry of Baudelaire (and the novels of Boileau and Narcejac), it is imbued with the spirit of Edgar Allan Poe. While the novel alludes to the Orpheus myth, the film recalls Poe's 'Ligeia' and its terrible epigraph: 'Man does not yield himself to the angels, nor to death utterly, save only through the weakness of his feeble will.'[40] The will in question is that of Ligeia, who returns from the dead by possessing the body of the narrator's second wife.

But Hitchcock is a filmmaker, so if we continue to operate on the assumption that artists must overcome their 'anxiety of influence' to create, we have to look elsewhere for his influences.

As usual there is nothing particularly hidden about Cecil B. DeMille's influence on *Vertigo*. DeMille, who believed in reincarnation all his life, had even made films about the possibility of what we would today call 'past-life therapy',[41] and *Vertigo* is a film about reincarnation. Ex-cop Scottie Ferguson (James Stewart) is hired to follow Madeleine (Kim Novak), the wife of an old friend, and falls in love with her. Seemingly possessed by the spirit of her ancestor Carlotta, who died by her own hand, she commits suicide the same way, by jumping off a bell tower. Then Scottie meets her seeming double, Judy (also played by Novak), and transforms her into the woman he loved and lost. Less visibly, and more profoundly, the supernatural elements in *Vertigo* also hark back to the Fritz Lang film that made Hitchcock want to make films,

Above and opposite page:
Kim Novak in *Vertigo* (1957).

even if he did his best to forget the director's name: *Der müde Tod*, in which a woman whose lover has died enters the Kingdom of Death to plead for his life, only to relive her loss in three successive reincarnations — just as Carlotta-Madeleine-Judy dies three times despite Scottie's efforts to save her.[42] Fritz Lang's Expressionist fairytale about Death and the Maiden is where Hitchcock first encountered the couple Persephone–Hades (Eros and Thanatos), and the high point of *Vertigo*'s ravishing Technicolor Expressionism is their paradoxical fusion. When Scottie turns Judy into Madeleine, the light from a neon sign outside the window, shot through a heavy diffusion filter, almost dissolves her image in a lime-green haze — the color of death in *Vertigo* — as she comes toward the camera.

If DeMille was Hitchcock's ego ideal, Lang was his superego, as is evident in *Rear Window*, where Jeffries, the neighbourhood Dr Mabuse,[43] almost pays the ultimate price for wanting to see and control everything in his little world. In *Vertigo* Lang supplied the cinematic source both for the dark fairytale and for its deconstruction, which oc-

curs when Scotty, who thinks he's in a ghost story, realizes he's actually in a film noir — a variation on Lang's great film noir *Scarlet Street* (1946), where a downtrodden clerk and Sunday painter becomes a real artist after falling in love with a tart, then murders her when he learns that she's been taking orders from her pimp all along. 'Pimp' is not a bad description of Scottie's school friend, oily Gavin Elster (Tom Helmore), who made Judy over to look like his wife and threw her in Scottie's arms as part of an insanely baroque scheme to murder the real Madeleine. When Scottie learns that Judy was a puppet in Elster's hands, he kills her by accident in a jealous rage.

Many interpretations of the ending of *Vertigo* are possible, including the supernatural one that Hitchcock's neighbour at Paramount would probably have preferred. But if it's true that an artist's deepest influences can't be revised away, Hitchcock's film expresses the hard wisdom of Lang, and of Poe as described by D. H. Lawrence, who could be talking about the uncanny images Saul Bass created for the opening credits: 'Poe wanted to know … what

Storyboards

Storyboards are synonymous with Alfred Hitchcock, but he did not invent them – ironically, he learned about them from David O. Selznick. The first live-action film to make extensive use of storyboards (a technique developed by Walt Disney) was *Gone with the Wind*, for which Selznick as producer gave art director William Cameron Menzies credit as 'production designer'. While Selznick frequently ignored Menzies' storyboards, he found them a valuable tool for extending his control of the filmmaking process to the actual filming of scenes, traditionally the director's domain.

No storyboard has ever turned up from Hitchcock's English period – he had always shown his collaborators how shots would look by doing little sketches, and would continue to do so in Hollywood. ('His way of communicating was to sit down and literally draw three lines and say, "Do you have the idea?" ' recalled Ted Haworth, the production designer for *Strangers on a Train*.) It is in these sketches, and not in detailed drawings executed by others, that we can see something Jean-Luc

Godard spoke of with respect to Hitchcock: the primacy of the hand as a creative tool.

However, beginning with *Foreign Correspondent*, on which Menzies is credited for 'special production effects', including the point-of-view plane-crash sequence, which Menzies had previously done in snow for Paul L. Stein's *The Lottery Bride* (1930). Storyboards were added to Hitchcock's arsenal. They might be discarded when a better idea suggested itself, but they were another tool for pre-visualization, which was important to his imaginative process. Perhaps this was a hangover from his Jesuit education, which would have taught him 'composition of the place' as part of the technique of meditation. St Ignatius of Loyola wrote in *The Spiritual Exercises*: 'When a contemplation or meditation is about something that can be gazed on, the composition consists of seeing in imagination the place where what I want to contemplate is taking place' – preferably with an abundance of physical details.

Storyboards also seem to have influenced Hitchcock's visual style. If *Rebecca* had been a gothic novel,

Foreign Correspondent was a graphic novel, and that reflects at least partly the influence of production drawings by Menzies and his collaborators. But all Hitchcock's films strive for the economy and strength of line that we are accustomed to seeing in commercial illustration, the subject he studied at art school. Truffaut said of *Notorious*: 'The ensemble is as precise as an animated cartoon.'

He brought that style to perfection with cameraman Robert Burks in *Strangers on a Train* and the twelve other films they made together. A fan of *Terry and the Pirates*, Hitchcock ordered the Warners research library to send up samples of comics drawn by Milton Caniff when he was starting production on that film. Storyboards would continue to influence the style of his films with Burks until one of the late ones actually turned into a storyboard for six shots – the sequence in *The Birds* that intercuts three quick close-ups of Tippi Hedren with images of a fire racing along the pavement to a car that explodes.

The uses of storyboards extended outside the production process.

Hitchcock could always point to them to promote the myth (of which Selznick was understandably sceptical) that he was an economical director because he pre-planned every shot. The storyboard was also a useful metaphor for teaching the press and the public that the images of a film should originate, already formed like Platonic ideas, in the mind of the director.

Eventually, Hitchcock ended up 'printing the legend'. In response to a request from the MGM publicity department, he had Mentor Heubner (who had done production sketches for *Strangers*) fabricate storyboards for the crop-dusting sequence in *North by Northwest* after it had already been shot. These drawings, despite the fact that they bore no resemblance to the actual sequence, became the most famous Hitchcock storyboards of all, a symbol of the director's sovereign power. Invented by the enemy, the storyboard in Hitchcock's hands had switched sides.

The plane sequence in *North By Northwest* (1959), in storyboard format (above) and in the film (opposite page).

76

Opposite page: Alfred Hitchcock and Cary Grant
on the set of *North By Northwest* (1959).

Above: Cary Grant and Eva Marie Saint
in North By Northwest (1959).

was the strangeness in the eyes of Ligeia. She might have told him it was horror … at being vampirized by his consciousness.'

A redemptive sequel

Although *The Paradine Case* featured a wicked Selznick-style femme fatale, those dark ladies — and other conventions of film noir — found their way belatedly into Hitchcock's cinema, where they are unconventionally cast as victims: Judy in *Vertigo*, Eve in *North by Northwest*, Marnie and even Marion Crane in *Psycho* behave like the seductive female criminals who usually propel this misogynistic genre, but Hitchcock always seems to be on their side.

His indulgent attitude is most surprising in the case of Eve (Eva Marie Saint), the seductive CIA counter-spy who blithely sends Roger Thornhill (Cary Grant) to his death in a South Dakota cornfield. When he survives the attack by a crop-

dusting plane and finds her keeping company with the suave Russian spy Vandamm (James Mason), Roger has every reason to hate her.

North by Northwest (1959), planned at the same time as *Vertigo* and filmed just after it, is a redemptive sequel that ends happily in a high place despite past betrayals. All this happens with the blessing of a CIA spymaster (Leo G. Carroll), whose bland assurances that Eve was acting out of patriotism cannot quite erase our recollection that she was just as willing as he was to sacrifice Roger for the sake of her own skin and the cause she is serving.

Roger and Eve are star-crossed lovers like the hero and heroine of Leonard Bernstein's updated *Romeo and Juliet*, but they are spared a tragic ending by the kind of magical dispensation common in musicals — a genre that was situated at the top of the box-office charts when Hitchcock made *North by Northwest* for MGM, the company that specialized in them.[44] His chase movies had always

'Hitch and his audience', by Jean Douchet

Let's assume that James Stewart comes down from the screen of *Rear Window*, takes a seat in the cinema and becomes one of us, a spectator. His voyeuristic appetites feed on the opening scene of *Psycho*: in the middle of the day, the camera intrudes into a bedroom whose blinds are drawn down. And in this bedroom a couple, on a bed, are kissing, embracing, demonstrating their strong physical attraction. From that moment on he feels frustrated. He'd like to 'see more' ...

The spectator's feelings towards Janet [Leigh] are a mixture of envy and contempt. A woman who agrees to visit this seedy hotel room, in mid-afternoon, in her provincial home town, is unworthy of respect. The spectator can therefore attribute to her his own worst motives, including his unconscious desire – which he dare not act on himself – to steal.

And in fact, when she returns to her office, Janet witnesses a large cash transaction. The spectator, who is starting to become bored with these scenes of everyday office life, is eager for something to happen. Then (why not?) Janet takes the money for herself ... Now she's on the road. A motor-cycle cop stops her ... We dearly want her to get away with it and we're rooting for her. But that altruistic thought is a cover for our own crime, which it is Janet Leigh's job to assume on our behalf. It hides a base desire behind a sympathetic front – a desire that will be gratified: the cop stops tailing her ...

Now that we (and hence Janet Leigh) have rejected the notion of rescue, she becomes prey to all kinds of wild thoughts. She's in the power of the forces of the night, and cannot bear bright lights ... So we're relieved when she checks into the motel. But the bizarre, mysterious quality of the place, and of its owner, arouse in us a feeling of vague anxiety. We sense danger, all the more since Janet Leigh is alone in this sinister place, alone in her bedroom, with its wide-open window, as she looks for a place to hide her money (our money). And since we have every reason to be afraid, her conversation with [Anthony] Perkins seems to go on too long. We want to see our fear justified. Our desire to 'see' will become even stronger: Perkins is like us, and he watches his guest undress. Is it going to be rape or theft? No, something much worse. Because our desire and fear do not yet know in which real object they should be invested; they are still hazy in our minds, and the form they will take is also unspecified – a kind of shadow, or ectoplasm ...

This 'form-force' then does its deed ... a deed which Perkins, the dutiful son, tries to blot out. And while he does, we see everything through his eyes. We watch him perform his grubby household chores ... Perkins tips everything into a slimy, stagnant pool. The car sinks half-way down in the water. 'Let it disappear', we say to ourselves. At last it sinks completely, irrevocably. We breathe a sigh of relief. We believe the darkness – or our unconscious – has swallowed up for good our complicity in the theft. But in order to reach that point, we've become accomplices in a crime ...

This is an extract from 'Hitch and his audience', *Cahiers du cinéma*, no. 113, November 1960.

Opposite page: Anthony Perkins (top); Janet Leigh and Mort Mills (bottom) in *Psycho* (1960).

been episodic, but *North by Northwest*'s set pieces are treated like self-contained musical numbers. Here we see him inventing the genre that would become Hollywood's surest bulwark against television: the action film, with its free-standing 'action sequences'. He seems to have found inspiration in Poe's 'The Pit and the Pendulum' for the three episodes where Roger's life is in danger: the drunken car ride that almost sends him off a cliff; the crop-duster sequence, where the danger descends from the sky with a back-and-forth motion like a deadly scythe; and the Mount Rushmore climax, with its breathless views of the abyss,[45] and a last-minute rescue by the forces of order.

Cinema and everyday life

Like Hitchcock, Walt Disney hosted a popular TV series each week, which permitted him to finance and publicize his crowning achievement, Disneyland. Now, with Lew Wasserman handling the negotiations, Hitchcock used the profits from his series to build his own Disneyland, *Psycho*, which he financed himself when Paramount rejected the project. As a result his most profitable film was made at Universal, where *Alfred Hitchcock Presents* had always been filmed. The move to Universal (which Wasserman's agency owned) would begin a new era, so the numbers on the licence plate of the car Marion Crane (Janet Leigh) buys to cover her tracks as she flees with the stolen $40,000 add up to his favourite number — thirteen.

There is no TV set in the room Marion takes on a rainy night at the Bates Motel — perhaps because *Psycho* (1960) seems to be happening inside one. The black-and-white minimalism of the visual style Hitchcock created with his TV crew and cameraman John Russell recalls the style of Universal horror films like *The Incredible Shrinking Man*, whose huge profits had caught his attention — a style hewn from the grey granite of 1950s TV. Hitchcock and Russell had already shot bits of *Psycho* in their telefilms, little experiments that helped shape this severely beautiful film, in which TV becomes cinema and everyday

Opposite page: the Norman Bates house in *Psycho* (1960).

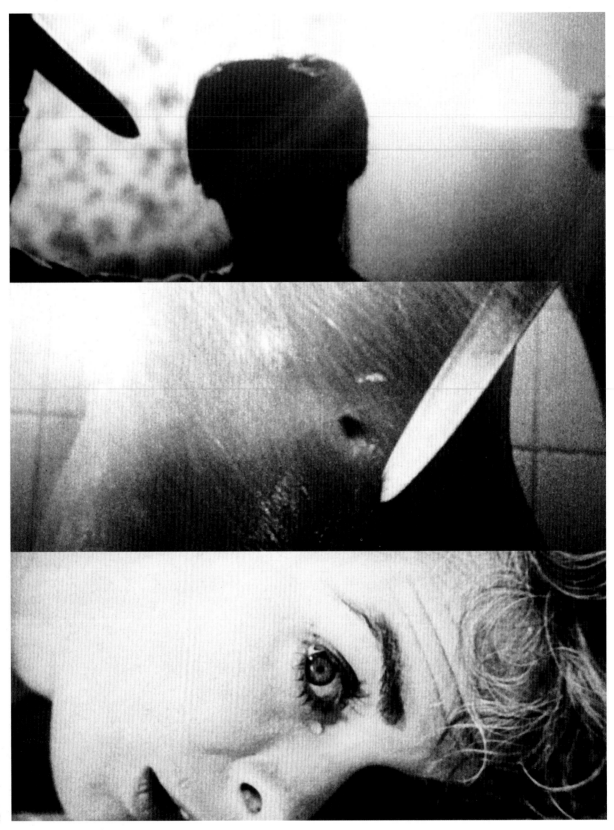

life becomes a fantastic vision out of Poe, *Psycho*
spawned another immensely lucrative genre, the
slasher film.

Although eventually two pans and a minia-
ture were used, *Psycho* was supposed to begin with a
high-tech variant on Hitchcock's signature camera
move: a 'four-mile dolly done with a helicopter'
that would have drifted through the window of the
Phoenix hotel room where Marion and Sam (John
Gavin) have just made love. Camera moves into the
screen re-enact the spatial violation that occurred
when D. W. Griffith's camera crossed the imaginary proscenium inscribed within the earliest film
images and created a grammar for telling stories by
cutting between various types of shot. Hitchcock's
camera loved to commemorate that event with
dangerous boundary crossings, like teleporting
through the plastic curtain to join Marion in the
shower. Indeed, shortly after the camera enters
the shower, the screen erupts in a montage of
knife-thrusts and body parts employing the whole
lexicon of shots — tight and medium close-ups,
inserts, medium shots, point-of-view shots, high
and low angles — that Griffith invented after his
camera invaded the unified wide shot that reproduced the space of the proscenium stage. Because
Hitchcock never forgot that the theatre evoked by
the earliest films was still hidden inside the film
image, the cutting up of Marion's body re-enacts
the sacrificial *sparagmos* (dismemberment) by
which the primal unity of the image was fragmen-
ted and cinema as we know it was born.

The shower sequence includes a striking
tribute to DeMille: the close-up of the shower-
curtain rings snapping as Marion, clutching the
curtain, collapses and dies. This image was first
used in the modern section of DeMille's 1923 *Ten
Commandments*, when the leper Sally Lung (Nita
Naldi, the star of Hitchcock's *The Mountain Eagle*)

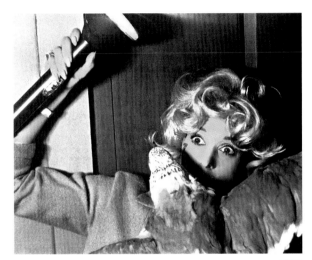

The murderous look
The Birds

Piqued by her encounter with Mitch Brenner in a San Francisco pet shop, playgirl Melanie Daniels has driven to his weekend residence in Bodega Day to deliver a pair of love-birds to him. To preserve the element of surprise, she has used a motorboat to approach his house from the lake side, and now she is returning to the dock she left from, where Mitch, having spotted her, is waiting, ready for the next phase of their romantic comedy to begin. But another type of movie begins when a gull comes out of nowhere and strikes Melanie on the head.

Her round trip on the lake has followed a strict pattern of alternation – shot of Melanie / shot of what she sees. In other words, the sequence, like the film of which it is a part, told mostly from Melanie's point of view, carries Hitchcock's style of subjective filmmaking as far as it can go. But at that point the meaning of the style is suddenly reversed.

When the gull enters the picture, Hitchcock told François Truffaut, he had to include objective shots of it before and after it strikes Melanie so that the audience wouldn't mistake the aggressor for 'a piece of paper that blew through the shot'. Coming where the pattern of alternation leads us to expect shots of Mitch, the gull is substituted for his concupiscent look and becomes a metaphor for it, as Raymond Bellour has argued in a classic structural analysis.

In later bird attacks, Hitchcock directed the audience's attention with a different device. The word 'Look' shouted off screen causes one of the characters to look away, and the beginning of the attack appears in the shot that shows what the character sees, as if the attack were being caused by her look.

Thus the film approaches the style of Fritz Lang, as described by Jean Douchet (*Cahiers du cinéma*, no. 103): 'Suspense in Lang is manifested in the eyes and never outside the characters … At the end of a shot the direction of the look … always announces that something is about to happen.' According to Jean-Pierre Oudart, the inventor of the concept of 'suture' that students of the cinema of shot–reverse shot have been using for the last forty years,

Hitchcock was profoundly influenced by the films of Fritz Lang, where each shot is the effect of the previous shot and the cause of the next, but he masked Lang's metaphysic with his own: the look and what is seen, the basic unit of all character relationships in a Hitchcock film.

In *The Birds* the cause-and-effect link, long repressed, peeps out from under the subjective editing, as if the birds were the physical embodiment of the looks of desire, jealousy and fear the characters direct at one another. This pattern, of which Hitchcock was no doubt unconscious, recalls a medieval allegory of lust that he probably never saw: birds flying out of someone's eyes and attacking the object of his desire.

Tippi Hedren and Rod Taylor
in *The Birds* (1963).

Following pages: Alfred Hitchcock with Veronica Cartwright, Rod Taylor, Tippi Hedren and Jessica Tandy on the set of *The Birds* (1963).

laughs at the villain's horror after she tells him she's given him her disease, then vanishes behind a curtain. He fires a gun through the curtain, she pulls it down as she dies, and DeMille prolongs the moment with three shots of the curtain rings snapping.[46] Hitchcock's reprise of the image of the rings when Marion is killed in the shower was his farewell to his former idol, who closed his office at Paramount at the beginning of 1959 and died a couple of weeks later, secure in the knowledge that his last picture, *The Ten Commandments* (1956), had grossed $80 million. But DeMille's use of special effects and even animation to portray the plagues visited by Charlton Heston (Moses) on Yul Brynner[47] (Rameses II) would have nothing on his star pupil's next film, based on a Daphne du Maurier story about an avian apocalypse that had first been dramatized on the radio show DeMille had created.

A prototype of the disaster film

This time it is at least plausible that there would be no TV in the home of Mitch Brenner (Rod Taylor), his mother Lydia (Jessica Tandy) and his little sister Cathy (Veronica Cartwright) — Lydia is enough of a snob to have banned it. But Cathy alludes to it when she tells their dinner guest Melanie Daniels ('Tippi' Hedren) about her brother's client who shot his wife for changing the channel while he was watching a baseball game. TV is the appropriate medium for the domestic murders portrayed in Hitchcock's series, but the movie we're watching will be vastly different in scale.

The Birds (1963) is the prototype of a new genre — the disaster film — that would pour millions of dollars into Universal's coffers in the 1970s. But Lew Wasserman made sure that *Earthquake* (1974) (which won an Oscar for Albert Whitlock, one of the key technicians on *The Birds*) avoided the errors that had kept Hitchcock's film from pleasing critics and audiences — he loaded it with stars (led by Charlton Heston) and saw to it that the filmmakers gave it a happy ending and a moral that a child could grasp.

Now a star himself, Hitchcock certainly had reason to think he could get away with using a no-name cast and offering no explanation for the bird attacks. After all, a lengthy trailer in which he spoke to the audience about humanity's relations with 'our feathered friends' (satirizing the delightfully pompous trailer DeMille had made for *The Ten Commandments*) would already have planted the idea that the birds in the film are avenging centuries of abuse. Audiences probably assumed that was the explanation, although the town drunk, quoting Ezekiel, suggests that this 'plague', as Mitch calls it, is of the Old Testament variety.

The promotional campaign deliberately raised expectations that are frustrated by the first 40 minutes of the film. When the birds belatedly erupt in spasms of mounting violence, they are pure projections of our bottled-up desire. Worse, our spectatorial sadism (which seems especially directed at children) is denounced by a hysterical mother who looks right at the camera as she addresses Melanie: 'I think you're the cause of this! I think you're *evil*!'

Headstrong heiress and tabloid celebrity Melanie Daniels is our surrogate. Her pursuit of Mitch Brenner turns into a daytime version of the transgressive journey into images shot by a second unit that ended in Marion Crane's murder by montage in the shower. Melanie's motorboat jaunt across a lake to the Brenner house (one of Albert Whitlock's matte paintings) to play a rather lame practical joke ends with the first bird attack — a seagull strikes her head as she approaches Mitch, who is waiting for her on the dock with a delicious promise of sexual payback in his eyes.

Successive attacks are interspersed with scenes in the cafe and the Brenner house, where the curtain goes up on Hitchcock's little theatre: rest periods permitting us to recharge our batteries with the violent impulses that made us purchase a ticket in the first place. This time the climax happens not in the bathroom or cellar, but in the attic, where open-beaked birds fly straight into the camera, until Melanie is reduced to a beautiful shell emptied by trauma: no longer seeing, only seen. Since the film would be over at this point, Hitchcock eliminated an ending where the family flees in Melanie's convertible pursued by a cloud of birds and escapes thanks to a miracle called down by Lydia reciting the Lord's Prayer. Instead he chose to end with an ambiguous miracle, a shot of the car parting a Red Sea of birds and vanishing in the distance, leaving behind a screen filled with cawing aggressors: our unsatisfied desires.

MR. HITCHCOCK

Sean Connery and Tippi Hedren
in *Marnie* (1964).

Marnie, *c'est moi*

Marnie (1964) was supposed to mark Grace Kelly's return to the screen. Having lured Cary Grant out of retirement by offering him the role of a jewel thief, Hitchcock planned to follow *Psycho* by doing the same thing with the Princess of Monaco. But the picture was delayed, first by the need to wait for Kelly, then by her decision to withdraw for reasons of state.[48] Later, in the course of working with his protégée Tippi Hedren on *The Birds*, Hitchcock decided that she could play the part.

But *Marnie* became, in Truffaut's words, 'a great flawed film' ('*un grand film malade*'), which he defines as 'a masterpiece that has been aborted', often by 'an excess of sincerity'. The diagnosis seems right. Hitchcock directed Hedren in both her films for him as no actress had ever been directed before, dictating each inflection and blink of an eye, projecting himself completely into her characters, and particularly into Marnie. This caused him to have anxiety attacks during the shooting of *The Birds*; during the shooting of Marnie it created disruptive tensions with Hedren like those in the film between Marnie and Mark (Sean Connery), a darker version of the character played by Grant in *Notorious*, who can only express his love through predatory behaviour. In this case Hitchcock's controlling behaviour seems to have been armour against the identification that propels the film: 'Marnie, *c'est moi*.'

Marnie is neurotic, phobic, frigid. (As a hint, Hitchcock confided in Jay Presson Allen, who wrote the script, that he was impotent.) She is also a master of disguise, someone from the wrong side of the tracks who has acquired a veneer of class that puts her betters to shame, and a brilliant thief. The wordless scenes where she is practising her métier are among the best Hitchcock ever filmed, and her anxiety attacks, nightmares and traumatic flashbacks are more emotional (and scarier) than anything in *Spellbound* or *Vertigo*. Surprisingly, her last scene with her mother (Louise Latham, in a problematic performance), after their transference of guilt has been resolved, is quite moving.

Producer John Houseman described Hitchcock in the 1940s as someone who still bore scars inflicted by the English class system, and one of the odd things about *Marnie* is its Englishness. 'We tell the mystery of this girl in a series of images[,] of pictures and settings and backgrounds', Hitchcock wrote to the production department, adding that the street where Marnie's mother lives, with a looming, oppressive steamship blocking the vanishing point, should be 'like a north of England town' (rather than the Cornish setting of Graham's novel).

The most striking shot in the film is the culmination of Hitchcock's experiments with widescreen formats: a very wide shot of Marnie robbing a safe, separated by a partition from an elderly cleaning woman mopping the floor a few feet away. This sets up a classic suspense sequence by giving the audience information Marnie doesn't have, but it is also a textbook image of two possible fates that await women in a society shaped by class and by sexism. The shot says that Marnie's thefts, like Hitchcock's films, are revolutionary acts,[49] even if she has to turn herself into 'a model employee' to pull them off — and even if they are committed by the sick heroine of a '*grand film malade*'.

Spies like me

When Hitchcock proposed to Lew Wasserman his cherished project of filming James M. Barrie's play *Mary Rose*, a period piece with Hedren playing a woman who is carried off by fairies, Wasserman

hated the idea. The failure of *Marnie* had shaken Hitchcock's confidence, so instead he ended up doing a spy film set behind the Iron Curtain, starring Paul Newman and Julie Andrews.

Torn Curtain (1966) suffers from the loss of Hitchcock's editor, George Tomasini, and Bernard Herrmann, whom Wasserman convinced the director to replace with a 'more contemporary' composer. But it is a beautiful, intelligent riposte to the James Bond films (cartoonish blockbusters spun off of *North By Northwest* that Wasserman no doubt had hoped Hitchcock would make better for his studio), and a prophetic one — the MacGuffin Newman steals, 'Gamma 5', gave Ronald Reagan the idea for the 'Star Wars' anti-missile programme.

Now Hitchcock began plotting a very experimental film about a serial killer, and had slides and test footage shot of anonymous actors in New York, using natural lighting. But the sexual frankness of the script scared Wasserman, who persuaded him to adapt a spy thriller by Leon Uris with a budget that permitted filming scenes on location in Europe. To avoid studio interference, Hitchcock shot *Topaz* (1969) while the script was being written.

Like *Torn Curtain*, *Topaz* has a protagonist who spends most of his time endangering people who are more likable than he is. Neither of these intrepid 'cold warriors' ever shows emotion, as if they were following Wasserman's orders to his old friend: 'Be cold. Do your job.'[50]

At the end of *Topaz* the hero fights a duel with a traitor who has slept with his wife, but his opponent is killed by a faceless sniper. This elegy for the codes of honour that shaped the moral universe of classical cinema provoked some titters during a preview, where fans of the jingoistic novel also expressed dislike for Hitchcock's icy denunciation of Cold War ethics.

Hitchcock filmed two new endings but refused to make cuts, so Wasserman used as his cat's paw a British distributor who wouldn't book the film without an interval for refreshment sales. Probably remembering the philistine distributor who almost buried *The Lodger*, Hitchcock yielded and let the studio mutilate *Topaz*, after which Wasserman told the distributor he could forget about his intermission.

Frenzy

Hitchcock's Universal contract said that he could make any film for $3 million as long as it wasn't *Mary Rose*. He now invoked that clause to make *Frenzy* (1972), based on a novel about a psychopathic strangler in contemporary London, which adopted the working title of his aborted serial killer film.

Made in Hitchcock's home town, far from the benevolent advice of his former agent, *Frenzy* is the work of a young man with the confident skills of an old master. The complex montage in the sequence showing Rusk (Barry Foster), the killer, wrestling with a corpse in the back of a moving potato truck brilliantly concludes the series of suspense sequences

without music that began with the mill in *Foreign Correspondent*. Literalism is the key to *Frenzy*'s modernity, expressed through a camera that remains objective for long stretches of time, using subjective editing mostly for shots of corpses or the ghastly meals cooked by the wife of the unfortunate Scotland Yard detective in charge of the case.

Talking to a writer about plans for the first *Frenzy*, Hitchcock described it as a prequel to *Shadow of a Doubt*, showing what Uncle Charlie had been up to before coming to Santa Rosa. As realized here, the death of the hero's ex-wife — a companion piece to the endless killing in the farmhouse in *Torn Curtain* — strips away the romance and symbolism of the Persephone myth with an unflinching, literal portrayal of rape and murder. That grimy literalness is Hitchcock's legacy to the flourishing gore cinema of today.

As in *The Lodger*, the audience is fooled into thinking that the innocent and very unlikable hero is the culprit, but shots of his hand bleeding or his foot crushing a box of grapes are devoid of any Christological connotations. Any hidden meanings in *Frenzy* are autobiographical: like Hitchcock's father, the charming killer played by Foster is a cockney wholesaler working in Covent Garden market who sends an innocent man to jail, re-enacting for the last time the trauma that marked Hitchcock when he was five years old.

The last shot of the last picture
Although critics described *Frenzy* as Hitchcock's testament, he surprised everyone by bringing the curtain down with *Family Plot* (1976), a comedy in the vein of *The Trouble with Harry*, whose intricate double plot features a séance ('a bit of *Mary Rose*',

he told a reporter[51]), transference of guilt and the kidnapping of a bishop in front of paralysed worshippers celebrating High Mass. *Family Plot* is a very modern-looking film, by turns cinema, TV series, comic book and amusement park ride — most of the sources for Hollywood cinema today.[52] DeMille may have invented Hollywood, but Hitchcock had re-invented it.

Impatient with delays during the first week of shooting, he discarded his storyboards and let the scenes he had blocked out on the set with his young actors dictate the camera moves. The first scene to be filmed this way was a high-angle shot of a detective following a reluctant witness through a labyrinth of paths in a cemetery before cornering and questioning her. This 'living Mondrian', as Hitchcock called it, diagrams the film's two plots: one about a black-clad criminal couple — Morticia and Gomez Addams, in effect,

although the character is called 'Adamson' — and one (see Jean Douchet) about a pair of game-show contestants who'll win $10,000 if they find them, which criss-cross without connecting and collide at the end. The soundtrack for the Mondrian is the distant words of a funeral service, and at the last minute Hitchcock, to confound his interpreters, dubbed in a text from the Book of Mormon.[53]

In truth, he simply enjoyed filmmaking too much to stop. A reporter on the set watched him direct the last scene, a crane shot showing a fake medium (Barbara Harris) apparently using psychic powers to locate a stolen diamond. The picture wrapped for lunch and the reporter left, satisfied that he'd seen Alfred Hitchcock film the last shot of his last picture. After lunch Hitchcock called everyone back to film Harris looking at the camera and winking.

Barbara Harris in *Family Plot* (1976).

Opposite page:
Barbara Leigh-Hunt in *Frenzy* (1972).

Chronology

1899

13 August. Born in Leytonstone, London. Alfred Joseph Hitchcock is the third child of William and Emma Hitchcock. He has a brother, William, and a sister, Ellen (Nellie). The father is a greengrocer, and the family lives in rooms over the shop.

1906

The Hitchcocks move to Limehouse, near the London docks.

1906–17

An avid reader in his youth, he discovers Poe (his favourite writer), Buchan, Chesterton and Flaubert. He also discovers film and theatre.

1910

Enters St Ignatius' College. He studies with the Jesuit fathers but continues to live at home.

1913

Enters London School of Engineering.

1914

Hired by W. T. Henley's Telegraphic Works, Hitchcock is popular with his fellow employees and edits the company newsletter, *The Henley Telegraph*. Death of his father.

1916

Enters Goldsmiths' College, where he studies commercial illustration.

Shooting of *The Thirty-Nine Steps* (1935) with Madeleine Carroll and his wife and frequent collaborator Alma Reville.

1917

Rents a flat in London. He is promoted to the advertising department at Henley's and learns about filmmaking by reading professional publications.

1920

Hitchcock sees J. M. Barrie's play *Mary Rose* about a young girl who is carried off by fairies. For the rest of his life he will dream of filming it.

1921

Hired by Famous Players-Lasky in Islington, first to write and draw intertitles, then as artistic director. He meets Alma Reville and studies screenwriting, with Jeanie Mac-Pherson, Cecil B. DeMille's muse, and other writers from Paramount.

1922

Famous Players closes. Hitchcock stays on at the Islington studio, making himself useful in various capacities. He writes screenplays, including a treatment, *Goodnight Nurse*, which was recently rediscovered and sold at auction.

1923

Production interrupted of *Number 13*, which would have been Hitchcock's first film as a director. He joins the Select Organization, directed by Michael Balcon. He becomes Graham Cutts's assistant director on five films and hires Alma Reville as his assistant.

In his first house in Hollywood in the 1940s.

Rehearsal with his daughter Patricia who plays a minor part in *Strangers on a Train* (1951).

1924

The Select Organization becomes Gainsborough Productions. Hitchcock works as an assistant on *The Blackguard*, co-produced by UFA in Berlin, where he meets F. W. Murnau and observes the shooting of *The Last Laugh* and very probably the shooting of Fritz Lang's *Der Nibelungen*.

1925

Promoted to director by Balcon, he makes two films in Munich: *The Pleasure Garden* and *The Mountain Eagle*, both written by Eliot Stannard, who would be the screenwriter of all his first films. On a ship in the middle of a storm he proposes marriage to Alma. He makes friends with the intellectuals of the London Film Society, in particular Ivor Montagu and Angus MacPhail, the inventor of the MacGuffin.

1926

Filming of *The Lodger*. The distributor C. M. Woolf refuses to take the film. Hired by Balcon to 're-edit' it, Ivor Montagu, without changing much, saves the film.

1927

The Lodger is a big success. Marriage to Alma. Announcement of Hitchcock's departure to British International Pictures. Obliged to remain at Gainsborough for a few more months, he makes *Downhill* and *Easy Virtue*. At BIP he makes *The Ring*, for which he is the only credited screenwriter (something that will never happen again). The start of his collaboration with cameraman Jack Cox, with whom he will make twelve films. Alma becomes pregnant.

Shooting of *Strangers on a Train* (1951): Patricia plays a senator's daughter.

1928

Birth of Patricia Hitchcock.

1929

Blackmail is filmed in two versions, silent and sound. Makes *Juno and the Paycock*, 'the first all-sound film by Hitchcock', a print of which is burned in a public square in Belfast.

1930

Hitchcock directs three episodes of *Elstree Calling*, a promotional film for BIP that traces what will be the cardinal points of Hitchcock's future career: theatre, cinema and television. *Murder!* is also filmed in a German version (*Mary*). Return to UFA in a country en route to fascism.

1931

Failure of the ambitious *Rich and Strange*.

1932

First contacts with Hollywood producers.

1934–38

Return to Islington studios, home of Michael Balcon's new company, British Gaumont Pictures. With Charles Bennett, Angus MacPhail and Ivor Montagu, he invents the Hitchcock thriller in *The Man Who Knew Too Much*, *The Thirty-Nine Steps*, *Young and Innocent* and *The Lady Vanishes*. International success despite a second run-in with the distributor C. M. Woolf over *The Man Who Knew Too Much*.

Cooking with Patricia in the 1950s.

1939–40
Moves to Hollywood. Filming of *Rebecca* and *Foreign Correspondent*. Selznick wins the Oscar for Best Picture for *Rebecca*.

1941
Oscar for Joan Fontaine for *Suspicion*.

1943–44
During the making of *Shadow of a Doubt*, Hitchcock's mother Emma dies in England. Makes two short propaganda films in England, *Bon Voyage* and *Aventure malgache* (Hitchcock's only French-language film), with the producer Sidney Bernstein, who will become his partner in 1948. He is visited at his hotel by Samuel Fuller, former journalist, writer and soldier. Hitchcock asks Fuller what he's doing in England. 'If I told you that,' growls Fuller, 'I'd have to kill you.'

1945
Second trip to England (in third class) to view images of the death camps and write a documentary, *Memory of the Camps*. The film is never screened and the last reel, about Auschwitz, is 'lost'.

1948–49
Films *Rope* and *Under Capricorn* for Transatlantic Pictures, the company he has created with Sidney Bernstein.

1950–54
Four films for Warner Bros. Patricia Hitchcock acts on film for the first time in *Stage Fright* and *Strangers on a Train*.

1953
Birth of Patricia Hitchcock O'Connell's first daughter, Mary Alma.

1954–56
Rear Window marks the beginning of his contract with Paramount and the first of four collaborations with the dialogue specialist John Michael Hayes.

1954
First encounter with the *Cahiers du cinéma* group during the filming of *To Catch a Thief* on the Riviera. Birth of Teresa O'Connell, his second granddaughter.

1955–63
The series *Alfred Hitchcock Presents* is on the air every week.

1957
Return to Warner Bros. for *The Wrong Man*. Vera Miles, who was supposed to star in *Vertigo*, gets pregnant and is replaced by Kim Novak.

1958
Alma Hitchcock, suffering from cancer, is cured thanks to an experimental treatment. April 13. 'Lamb to the Slaughter' is broadcast, starring Barbara Bel Geddes — the most famous episode of *Alfred Hitchcock Presents*.

1959
Hitchcock appears in *Tactic*, an educational broadcast about cancer that he 'directs' on-camera as a specialist in fear. *North by Northwest* is a blockbuster for MGM. Birth of Kathleen O'Connell, his third granddaughter.

1960
Since Paramount doesn't understand Hitchcock's desire to make *Psycho*, a morbid novel by a lurid writer, he finances the film with revenues from his TV series and films it with his TV crew. The film is a big success to the astonishment of everyone, Hitchcock included.

1962–66
Takes up residence at Universal, becomes a stockholder and surrounds himself with a solid team of collaborators for *The Birds* and *Marnie*. His long-time editor George Tomasini dies of a heart attack; Hitchcock is alienated from his protégée Tippi Hedren because of personal differences; his cameraman, Robert Burks, doesn't come back for *Torn Curtain* because Hitchcock wants to shoot more scenes than ever using back projection.

1963
Interviewed by François Truffaut for *Hitchcock*; sends a copy of *The Birds* to Truffaut to be screened for Jean Cocteau, who is dying.

1968
Receives the Irving Thalberg Award, the only 'personal' Oscar Hitchcock ever received.

1968–72
Topaz bombs, but Hitchcock recovers his box-office standing by making *Frenzy* in London – it makes more money than *Psycho*.

1971
Becomes Chevalier of the Legion d'Honneur.

1974
Heart attack.
Has a pacemaker implanted.

1975–76
Making and triumphal release of his last film, *Family Plot*. Shortly after that, Alma suffers a severe stroke.

1976–79
Works on the screenplay and pre-production of *The Short Night*, but his health doesn't permit him to make the film.

1979
Receives the Lifetime Achievement Award of the American Film Institute. Is knighted by the Queen.

1980
29 April. Death of Alfred Hitchcock.

1982
6 July. Death of Alma Hitchcock.

A Pharaonic profile.

Alfred Hitchcock, Alma Reville and their daughter Patricia on the set of *Psycho* (1960).

At work with Alma Reville in the 1960s.

In front of a portrait of his daughter by the painter Nicole Kidman in the 1960s.

Alma Reville in the kitchen of the Bellagio road house in the 1970s.

Filmography

The Pleasure Garden 1925
B&W. Silent. **Screenplay** Eliot Stannard, based on a novel by Oliver Sandys. **Cinematography** Gaetano Di Ventimiglia. **Production** Emelka. **Running time** 1h 03. With Virginia Valli (Patsy Brand), Carmelita Geraghty (Jill Cheyne), Miles Mander (Levet), John Stuart (Hugh Fielding).
• Jill and Patsy, two chorus girls at The Pleasure Garden, marry two friends who leave for the tropics on business. When Patsy joins her husband, she finds that he has a native lover.

The Mountain Eagle 1926
B&W. Silent. **Screenplay** Eliot Stannard. **Cinematography** Gaetano Di Ventimiglia. **Production** Gainsborough Pictures, Emelka. **Running time** 57 m. With Bernard Goetzke (Pettigrew), Nita Naldi (Béatrice), Malcolm Keen (Fear O'God), John Hamilton (Edward Pettigrew).
• The Justice of the Peace in a mountain village harasses a young teacher with whom he obsessed. She seeks refuge in the hut of a hermit.

The Lodger, A Story of The London Fog 1926
B&W. Silent. **Screenplay** Eliot Stannard, based on a novel by Marie-Adelaide Belloc-Lowndes. **Cinematography** Gaetano Di Ventimiglia. **Production** Gainsborough Pictures. **Running time** 1h 14. With Ivor Novello (The Lodger), Malcolm Keen (Joe Betts), June (Daisy Bunting), Arthur Chesney (Mr Bunting), Marie Ault (Mrs Bunting).
• Mrs Bunting suspects her mysterious lodger of being The Avenger, a serial killer of young women.

Downhill 1927
B&W. Silent. **Screenplay** Eliot Stannard, based on a play by David LeStrange (pseudonym of Ivor Novello and Constance Collier). **Cinematography** Claude McDonnell. **Production** Gainsborough Pictures. **Running time** 1h 20. With Ivor Novello (Roddy Berwick), Robin Irvine (Tim Wakeley), Isabel Jeans (Julia).
• A student, accused of trifling with the affections of a shop girl, is thrown out of college and disinherited by his father, but he is protecting a friend who the real guilty party.

Easy Virtue 1927
B&W. Silent. **Screenplay** Eliot Stanwnard, based on a play by Noel Coward. **Cinematography** Claude McDonnell. **Production** Gainsborough Pictures. **Running time** 1h. With Isabel Jeans (Larita Filton), Franklin Dyall (John Filton), Eric Bransby Williams (Claude Robson).
• Larita marries the son of a wealthy family who know nothing about her scandalous past, but the young man's mother finds out and seeks to break up the marriage.

The Ring 1927
B&W. Silent. **Screenplay** Alfred Hitchcock. **Cinematography** Jack E. Cox. **Production** British International Pictures. **Running time** 1h 50. With Carl Brisson (Jack Sanders), Lillian Hall-Davies (Nelly), Ian Hunter (Bob Corby), Harry Terry (The Showman), Gordon Harker (Jack's Trainer).
• Two boxers, one a wealthy champion and the other just starting his career, are in love with the same woman.

The Farmer's Wife 1928
B&W. Silent. **Screenplay** Alfred Hitchcock, Eliot Stannard, based on a play by Eden Phillpotts. **Cinematography** Jack E. Cox. **Production** British International Pictures. **Running time** 1h 34. With Jameson Thomas (Sam Sweetland), Lillian Hall-Davies (Araminta Dench), Gordon Harker (Churdles Ash).
• A widowed farmer proposes to three unsuitable women, who luckily refuse him, then realizes that his pretty servant, who has helped him in his matrimonial misadventures, is secretly in love with him.

Champagne 1928
B&W. Silent. **Screenplay** Eliot Stannard, Alfred Hitchcock, based on an original subject by Walter C. Mycroft. Cinematography Jack E. Cox. **Production** British International Pictures. **Running time** 1h 44. With Betty Balfour (Betty), Gordon Harker (Betty's Father), Theo von Alten (The Man).
• A rich man convinces his madcap daughter that they are ruined so that she will have to take a job and learn some common sense.

The Manxman 1929
B&W. Silent. **Screenplay** Eliot Stannard, based on a short story by Hall Caine. **Cinematography** Jack E. Cox. **Production** British International Pictures. **Running time** 1h 44. With Carl Brisson (Pete Quilliam), Malcolm Keen (Philip Christian), Anny Ondra (Kate Cregeen), Randle Ayrton (Mr Cregeen), Clare Greet (Mrs Cregeen).
• Pete leaves the fishing village where he grew up to make his fortune, so he can return and marry Kate. When they hear of Pete's death, Kate and Philip, Pete's best friend, admit their love. Then Pete returns and marries Kate, who is carrying Philip's child.

Blackmail 1929
B&W. **Screenplay** Benn W. Levy, Alfred Hitchcock, based on a play by Charles Bennett. **Cinematography** Jack E. Cox. **Production** British International Pictures. **Running time** 1h 23. With Anny Ondra (Alice White), Cyril Ritchard (Crewe), John Longden (Frank Webber), Sara Allgood (Mrs White).
• A police detective investigating the murder of a painter learns that the murderer is his own fiancée. He conceals her crime, but they become the prey of a blackmailer. (This film exists in both silent and sound versions, made simultaneously.)

Juno And The Paycock 1929
B&W. Screenplay Alma Reville, Alfred Hitchcock, based on a play by Sean O'Casey. **Cinematography** Jack E. Cox. **Production** British International Pictures. **Running time** 1h 25. With Sara Allgood (Juno Boyle), Edward Chapman (Captain Boyle), John Laurie (Johnny Boyle), Marie O'Neill (Maisie Madigan).
• In Dublin, during the Irish Revolution, a poor family learn that they are to receive an inheritance.

Murder! 1930
B&W. **Screenplay** Alma Reville, Alfred Hitchcock, Walter Mycroft, based on Enter Sir John by Clemence Dane and Helen Simpson. **Cinematography** Jack E. Cox. **Production** British International Pictures. **Running time** 1h 32. With Herbert Marshall (Sir John), Norah Baring (Diana Baring), Edward Chapman (Ted Markham).
• Sir John, a famous actor-producer from the London stage, serves on the jury in a murder case. When an innocent girl is condemned to hang despite all his arguments, he decides to turn detective and go in search of the real murderer. (Hitchcock directed a German-language remake of Murder! in 1931.)

The Skin Game   1931

B&W. **Screenplay** Alma Reville, Alfred Hitchcock, based on a play by John Galsworthy. **Cinematography** Jack E. Cox. **Production** British International Pictures. **Running time** 1h 25. With Edmund Gwenn (Mr Hornblower), Jill Esmond (Jill Hillcrist), John Longden (Charles Hornblower), C. V. France (Mr Hillcrist), Helen Haye (Mrs Hillcrist).

• Old money and new money clash in an English village over the sale of a parcel of land.

Rich And Strange   1932

B&W. **Screenplay** Alma Reville, Alfred Hitchcock, Val Valentine based on an idea by Dale Collins. **Cinematography** Jack E. Cox. **Production** British International Pictures. **Running time** 1h 23. With Henry Kendall (Fred Hill), Joan Barry (Emily Hill), Percy Marmont (Commander Gordon), Betty Amann (The Princess), Elsie Randolph (The Old Maid).

• A bored white-collar worker and his wife use an inheritance to sail off in search of adventure in the China Seas, and find it.

Number Seventeen   1932

B&W. **Screenplay** Alma Reville, Alfred Hitchcock, Rodney Ackland, based on a play by J. Jefferson Farjeon. **Cinematography** Jack E. Cox. **Production** British International Pictures. **Running time** 1h 03. With Leon M. Lion (Ben), Anne Grey (Nora Brant), John Stuart (Detective Barton), Donald Carlthrop (Brant), Barry Jones (Henry Doyle), Garry Marsh (Shelldrake).

• Various mysterious characters meet in an old dark house that is being used as a rendezvous point for a gang of jewel thieves.

Waltzes From Vienna   1933

B&W. **Screenplay** Alma Reville, Guy Bolton, based on a play by A. M. Willner, Heinz Reichert and Ernst Marischka. **Cinematography** Glen McWilliam. **Production** Gaumont British Picture. **Running time** 1h 20. With Jessie Matthews (Rasi), Esmond Knight (Schani Strauss), Frank Vosper (Count Gustav von Stahl), Edmund Gwenn (Johann Strauss, the Elder), Fay Compton (Countess Helga von Stahl), Robert Hale (Ebeseder), Hindle Edgar (Leopold), Marcus Barron (Dreschler), Charles Heslop (Valet).

• Johann Strauss, Jr, lives in the shadow of his father, the great composer. A beautiful countess wants to help launch his composing career, but what will his fiancée say when she finds out?

The Man Who Knew Too Much   1934

B&W. **Screenplay** A. R. Rawlinson, Edwin Greenwood, Emlyn Williams, based on an original idea by D. B. Wyndham Lewis and Charles Bennett. **Cinematography** Curt Courant. **Production** Gaumont British Picture. **Running time** 1h 24. With Leslie Banks (Bob Lawrence), Peter Lorre (Abbott), Edna Best (Jill Lawrence), Frank Vosper (Ramon), Hugh Wakefield (Clive), Pierre Fresnay (Louis Bernard).

• An English couple vacationing in Switzerland learn of a plot to assassinate a visiting dignitary in London, but they can tell no one what they know because the plotters have kidnapped their teenage daughter to ensure their silence.

The Thirty-Nine Steps 1935

B&W. **Screenplay** Charles Bennett, Ian Hay, based on a novel by John Buchan. **Cinematography** Bernard Knowles. **Production** Gaumont British Picture. **Running time** 1h 21. With Robert Donat (Richard Hannay), Madeleine Carroll (Pamela), Lucie Mannheim (Annabella Smith), Godfrey Tearle (Professor Jordan), Peggy Ashcroft (Margaret), John Laurie (John).

• A Canadian new to London, Richard Hannay, becomes ensnared in an espionage plot. Wanted for murder by the police, he has to find the spy ring, and prove his innocence, especially to the charming Pamela, to whom he ends up accidentally handcuffed.

Secret Agent   1936

B&W. **Screenplay** Charles Bennett, Tan Hay, Jesse Lasky, Jr, based on a play by Campbell Dixon, based on Ashenden, by W. Somerset Maugham. **Cinematography** Bernard Knowles. **Production** Gaumont British Picture. **Running time** 1h 23. With Madeleine Carroll (Elsa), John Gielgud (Ashenden), Peter Lorre (The General), Robert Young (Marvin), Percy Marmont (Mr Caypor), Florence Kahn (Mrs Caypor), Lilli Palmer (Lilli).

• A British secret agent sent to Switzerland to assassinate a German spy he has never seen accidentally kills an innocent tourist.

Sabotage   1936

B&W. **Screenplay** Charles Bennett, Alma Reville, Ian Hay, Helen Simpson, based on a novel by Joseph Conrad (The Secret Agent). **Cinematography** Bernard Knowles. **Production** Gaumont British Picture. **Running time** 1h 16. With Sylvia Sydney (Mrs Verloc), Oscar Homolka (Mr Verloc), Desmond Tester (Stevie), John Loder (Ted), Joyce Barbour (Renée), Matthew Boulton (Superintendent Talbot), S. J. Warmington (Hollingshead), William Dewhurst (Professor A. F. Chatman).

• Mr Verloc, the owner of a cinema in London's East End, is a terrorist in the employ of a foreign government, but his young wife and brother-in-law know nothing about his activities.

Young And Innocent   1937

B&W. **Screenplay** Charles Bennett, Edwin Greenwood, Anthony Armstrong, Gerald Savary, based on A Shilling for Candles, by Josephine Tey. **Cinematography** Bernard Knowles. **Production** Gainsborough Pictures, Gaumont British Picture. **Running time** 1h 20. With Derrick de Marney (Robert Tisdall), Nova Pilbeam (Erica Burgoyne), Percy Marmont (Colonel Burgoyne), Edward Rigby (Old Will), Mary-Clare (Erica's Aunt), John Longden (Detective Inspector Kent).

• A young man is falsely accused of strangling a movie star who was apparently keeping him. He escapes from the police station and sets out to prove his innocence, helped by the Chief Constable's daughter.

The Lady Vanishes   1938

B&W. **Screenplay** Sidney Gilliat, Frank Launder, based on The Wheel Spins, by Ethel Lina White. **Cinematography** Jack E. Cox. **Production** Gainsborough Pictures. **Running time** 1h 37. With Margaret Lockwood (Iris Henderson), Michael Redgrave (Gilbert), Paul Lukas (Dr Hertz), Dame May Whitty (Miss Froy), Googie Withers (Blanche), Cecil Parker (Mr Todhunter).

• On a train a young English girl is befriended by an old lady who then vanishes, and no passenger will admit that the lady ever existed.

Jamaica Inn   1939

B&W. **Screenplay** Sidney Gilliat, Joan Harrison, J. B. Priestley, based on a novel by Daphne du Maurier. **Cinematography** Bernard Knowles. **Production** Mayflower Pictures. **Running time** 1h 48. With Maureen O'Hara (Mary), Charles Laughton (Sir Humphrey Pengallan), Leslie Banks (Joss Merlyn), Robert Newton (Jem Trehearne), Emlyn Williams (Harry), Marie Ney (Patience Merlyn).

• An orphan goes to live with her

aunt, whose husband owns a tavern used by shipwreckers for their murderous business.

Rebecca 1940
B&W. **Screenplay** Robert E. Sherwood, Joan Harrison, Philip McDonald, Michael Hogan, based on a novel by Daphne du Maurier. **Cinematography** George Barnes. **Production** Selznick Production. **Running time** 2h 10. With Laurence Olivier (Maxim de Winter), Joan Fontaine (Mrs de Winter), George Sanders (Jack Favell), Judith Anderson (Mrs Danvers).
• A timid girl marries the brooding owner of Manderley, a great house haunted by the memory of her husband's deceased first wife, the beautiful, mysterious Rebecca.

Foreign Correspondent 1940
B&W. **Screenplay** Charles Bennett, Joan Harrison, James Hilton, Robert Benchley. **Cinematography** Rudolph Maté. **Production** United Artists. Running time 2h. With Joel McCrea (Johnny Jones and Huntley Haverstock), Larayne Day (Carol Fisher), Herbert Marshall (Stephen Fisher), George Sanders (Scott Folliott).
• An American journalist new to the world of political intrigue witnesses the murder of a diplomat by Nazi agents in Holland, but when he pursues the killers he finds out that the real diplomat has been kidnapped.

Mr. And Mrs. Smith 1941
B&W. **Screenplay** Norman Krasna. **Cinematography** Harry Stradling. **Production** RKO. **Running time** 1h 35. With Carole Lombard (Ann), Robert Montgomery (David), Gene Raymond (Jeff Custer), Jack Carson (Chuck), Philip Merivale (Mr Custer), Lucile Watson (Mrs Custer).
• When a happily married couple discover that they aren't really mar-

ried, suspicion and jealousy rear their heads.

Suspicion 1941
B&W. **Screenplay** Samson Raphaelson, Joan Harrison, Alma Reville, based on *Before the Fact*, by Francis Iles. **Cinematography** Harry Stradling. **Production** RKO. **Running time** 1h 39. With Cary Grant (John Aysgarth), Joan Fontaine (Lina McLaidlaw), Sir Cedric Hardwicke (General McLaidlaw), Nigel Bruce (Beaky), May Whitty (Mrs McLaidlaw), Isabel Jeans (Mrs Newsham), Heather Angel (Ethel).
• Lina, a shy English girl, suspects her dashing husband of wanting to kill her for her inheritance.

Saboteur 1942
B&W. **Screenplay** Peter Viertel, Joan Harrison, Dorothy Parker, based on an original subject by Alfred Hitchcock. **Cinematography** Joseph Valentine. **Production** Universal Pictures. **Running time** 1h 48. With Robert Cummings (Barry Kane), Priscilla Lane (Pat), Otto Kruger (Tobin), Alan Baxter (Freeman), Clem Bevans (Neilson), Norman Lloyd (Fry), Alma Kruger (Mrs Sutton), Vaughan Glazer (Mr Miller).
• A worker in a munitions plant is falsely accused of sabotage and sets out on a cross-country search for the real saboteur.

Shadow Of A Doubt 1943
B&W. **Screenplay** Thornton Wilder, Alma Reville, Sally Benson, based on an original subject by Gordon McDonnell. **Cinematography** Joseph Valentine. **Production** Universal Skirball Productions. **Running time** 1h 48. With Joseph Cotten (Charles Oakley), Teresa Wright (Charlie Newton), MacDonald Carey (Jack Graham), Henry Travers (Joe Newton), Hume Cronyn (Herb Hawkins), Patricia Collinge (Emma Newton).
• Charles Oakley decides to spend

some time with his sister's family in the small town where he grew up. But his young niece begins to suspect that he is the killer of wealthy widows being sought by the police.

Lifeboat 1944
B&W. **Screenplay** Jo Swerling, based on an original subject by John Steinbeck. **Cinematography** Glen MacWilliams. **Production** 20th Century Fox. **Running time** 1h 36. With Tallulah Bankhead (Connie Porter), William Bendix (Gus Smith), Walter Slezak (Willie), Mary Anderson (Alice), John Hodiak (Kovac), Henry Hull (Charles Rittenhaus).
• In a lifeboat in the open sea, survivors of a ship sunk by the Nazis pick up the captain of the submarine that attacked them.

Spellbound 1945
B&W. **Screenplay** Ben Hecht, Angus MacPhail, Hilary St George Saunders, John Palmer, based on *The House of Dr. Edwardes*, by Francis Beeding. **Cinematography** George Barnes. **Production** Selznick International. **Running time** 1h 41. With Ingrid Bergman (Constance Peterson), Gregory Peck (John Ballantine), Rhonda Fleming (Mary Carmichael), Leo G. Carroll (Dr Murchison), Michael Chekhov (Dr Brulov).
• Dr Constance Peterson falls in love with the new director of the mental hospital where she works. But is he the real Dr Edwardes, or his murderer?

Notorious 1946
B&W. **Screenplay** Ben Hecht, based on an original subject by Alfred Hitchcock. **Cinematography** Ted Tetzlaff. **Production** RKO. **Running time** 1h 42. With Ingrid Bergman (Alicia Huberman), Cary Grant (T. R. Devlin), Claude Rains (Alexander Sebastian), Louis Calhern (Paul Prescott), Leopoldine Konstantin

(Mme Sebastian).
• An FBI agent falls in love with the woman he has enlisted to infiltrate a Nazi organization in Rio de Janeiro just after the war. But Sebastian, the chief Nazi, also falls for her and proposes marriage.

The Paradine Case 1947
B&W. **Screenplay** David O. Selznick, Alma Reville, based on a novel by Robert Hichens. **Cinematography** Lee Garmes. **Production** Selznick International. **Running time** 2h 05. With Gregory Peck (Anthony Keane), Ann Todd (Gay Keane), Charles Laughton (Judge Horfield), Charles Coburn (Simon Flaquer), Ethel Barrymore (Sophie Horfield), Louis Jourdan (André Latour), Alida Valli (Mrs Paradine).
• Barrister Anthony Keane falls in love with the beautiful Mrs Paradine, the client he is defending on a murder charge.

Rope 1948
Screenplay Arthur Laurents, Hume Cronyn, based on a play by Patrick Hamilton (*Rope's End*). **Cinematography** Joseph Valentine. **Production** Transatlantic Pictures. **Running time** 1h 20. With James Stewart (Rupert Cadell), John Dall (Brandon), Farley Granger (Phillip), Joan Chandler (Janet), Sir Cedric Hardwicke (Mr Kentley), Constance Collier (Mrs Atwater), Edith Evanson (Mrs Wilson), Douglas Dick (Kenneth), Dick Hogan (David Kentley).
• Two students murder a schoolmate and hide the body in a chest in their living room, where they are going to have a dinner party that evening for the victim's friends and family.

Under Capricorn 1949
Screenplay James Bridie, Hume Cronyn, based on a novel by Helen Simpson. **Cinematography** Jack Cardiff. **Production** Transatlantic Pictures. **Running time** 1h 57.

With Ingrid Bergman (Henrietta Flusky), Joseph Cotton (Sam Flusky), Michael Wilding (Charles Adare), Margaret Leighton (Milly), Jack Watling (Winter).

• In nineteenth-century Australia the governor's nephew falls in love with Hattie, the wife of a man who was once transported as punishment for murder. But Hattie, alcoholic and terrorized by her housekeeper, is hiding a terrible secret.

Stage Fright 1949
B&W. **Screenplay** Whitfield Cook, Alma Reville, based on a novel by Selwyn Jepson. **Cinematography** Wilkie Cooper. **Production** Warner Bros., First National. **Running time** 1h 50. With Marlene Dietrich (Charlotte Inwood), Jane Wyman (Eve Gill), Michael Wilding (Wilfred 'Ordinary' Smith), Richard Todd (Jonathan Cooper), Alistair Sim (Commodore Gill), Patricia Hitchcock (Chubby Banister).

• Charlotte Inwood, a theatre star, implicates an innocent man in a murder she committed. His fiancée, Eve, undertakes an investigation to clear his name.

Strangers on a Train 1951
B&W. **Screenplay** Raymond Chandler, Czenzi Ormonde, Whitfield Coo, based on a novel by Patricia Highsmith. **Cinematography** Robert Burks. **Production** Warner Bros. **Running time** 1h 41. With Farley Granger (Guy Haines), Robert Walker (Bruno Anthony), Ruth Roman (Anne Morton), Leo G. Carroll (Senator Morton), Patricia Hitchcock (Barbara Morton).

• On a train, tennis pro Guy Haines meets an admirer named Bruno, who proposes an exchange: Bruno will kill Guy's ex-wife and Guy will kill Bruno's father. Guy puts him off with a joke, which Bruno, who is insane, takes seriously.

I Confess 1953
B&W. **Screenplay** George Tabori, William Archibald, based on a play by Paul Anthelme (*Nos deux consciences*). **Cinematography** Robert Burks. **Production** Warner Bros. **Running time** 1h 35. With Montgomery Clift (Michael Logan), Anne Baxter (Ruth Grandfort), Karl Malden (Inspector Larrue), Brian Aherne (Willy Robertson), O. E. Hasse (Otto Keller).

• Otto Keller confesses to Father Logan that he has committed murder. Bound by the law of the confessional, Logan can't reveal the killer's identity when he himself is accused of the crime.

Dial M for Murder 1954
Screenplay Frederick Knott, based on his own play. **Cinematography** Robert Burks. **Production** Warner Bros. **Running time** 1h 28. With Ray Milland (Tony Wendice), Grace Kelly (Margot Wendice), Robert Cummings (Mark Halliday), John Williams (Chief Inspector Hubbard).

• A former tennis star, fearing that his rich wife is going to leave him, blackmails an old school chum into killing her.

Rear Window 1954
Screenplay John Michael Haynes, based on a short story by Cornell Woolrich. **Cinematography** Robert Burks. **Production** Paramount, Patron Inc. **Running time** 1h 42. With James Stewart (L. B. Jeffries), Grace Kelly (Lisa Fremont), Wendell Corey (Tom Doyle), Thelma Ritter (Stella), Raymond Burr (Lars Thorwald).

• A photojournalist, confined to his apartment with a broken leg staves off boredom by spying on his neighbours. Convinced that a murder has been committed in one of the apartments in the building across the courtyard, he enlists the help of his girlfriend to catch the killer.

To Catch a Thief 1954
Screenplay John Michael Hayes, based on a novel by David Dodge. **Cinematography** Robert Burks. **Production** Paramount. **Running time** 1h 37. With Cary Grant (John Robie), Grace Kelly (Francie Stevens), Charles Vanel (Bertrani), Jessie Royce Landis (Jessie Stevens).

• A retired burglar, John Robie, a.k.a. 'The Cat', has to clear his name when a copycat thief starts stealing jewels on the Riviera.

The Trouble with Harry 1956
Screenplay John Michael Hayes, based on a novel by J. Trevor Story. **Cinematography** Robert Burks. **Production** Paramount, Alfred Hitchcock Productions. **Running time** 1h 39. With Edmund Gwenn (Captain Albert Wiles), John Forsythe (Sam Marlowe), Shirley MacLaine (Jennifer Rogers), Mildred Natwick (Miss Gravely), Mildred Dunnock (Mrs Wiggs), Jerry Mathers (Arnie).

• A corpse named Harry turns up in an idyllic autumn forest, where several characters have reason to think that they killed him.

The Man Who Knew Too Much 1956
Screenplay John Michael Hayes, based on an original subject by Charles Bennett and D. B. Wyndham-Lewis. **Cinematography** Robert Burks. **Original Music** Bernard Herrmann. **Production** Paramount, Filwite Productions. **Running time** 2h. With James Stewart (Dr Ben McKenna), Doris Day (Jo McKenna), Daniel Gélin (Louis Bernard).

• Remake of Hitchcock's 1934 film of the same name.

The Wrong Man 1956
B&W. **Screenplay** Maxwell Anderson, Angus McPhail, based on a novel by Maxwell Anderson (*The True Story of Christopher Emmanuel Balestrero*). **Cinematography** Robert Burks. **Production** Warner Bros. **Running time** 1h 45. With Henry Fonda (Christopher Emmanuel Balestrero), Vera Miles (Rose Balestrero), Anthony Quayle (Frank O'Connor).

• A musician is arrested because of a chance resemblance to a hold-up man.

Vertigo 1957
Screenplay Alec Coppel, Samuel Taylor, based on a novel by Pierre Boileau and Thomas Narcejac (*D'entre les morts*). **Cinematography** Robert Burks. **Original Music** Bernard Herrmann. **Production** Paramount, Alfred Hitchcock Productions. **Running time** 2h. With James Stewart (John 'Scottie' Ferguson), Kim Novak (Madeleine Elster and Judy Barton), Barbara Bel Geddes (Midge Wood), Tom Helmore (Gavin Elster).

• Scottie, a detective who suffers from fear of heights, is hired by an old friend to follow his wife, Madeleine, who has been acting strangely.

North By Northwest 1959
Screenplay Ernest Lehman. **Cinematography** Robert Burks. **Original Music** Bernard Herrmann. **Production** Metro Goldwyn Mayer. **Running time** 2h 16. With Cary Grant (Roger Thornhill), Eva Marie Saint (Eve Kendall), James Mason (Phillip Vandamm), Jessie Royce Landis (Clara Thornhill), Leo G. Carroll (The Professor), Martin Landau (Leonard).

• Spies mistake advertising executive Roger Thornhill for a mystery man named George Kaplan. Pursued by both the police and the bad guys, Thornhill embarks on a cross-country search for Kaplan that lands him in the sleeping compartment of the beautiful Eve Kendall.

Psycho   **1960**
B&W. **Screenplay** Joseph Stefano, based on a novel by Robert Bloch. **Cinematography** John L. Russel. **Original Music** Bernard Herrmann. **Production** Paramount, Shamley Productions. **Running time** 1h 50. With Anthony Perkins (Norman Bates), Janet Leigh (Marion Crane), Vera Miles (Lila Crane), John Gavin (Sam Loomis), Patricia Hitchcock (Caroline). Martin Balsam (Milton Arbogast),
• Marion flees after stealing $40,000 from her boss. In a downpour at night, she stops at an out-of-the-way motel belonging to a young man who lives with his mother.

The Birds   **1963**
Screenplay Evan Hunter, based on a short story by Daphne du Maurier. **Cinematography** Robert Burks. **Original Music** Remi Gassman, Oskar Sala, Bernard Herrmann. **Production** Universal, Alfred Hitchcock Productions. **Running time** 2h. With Tippi Hedren (Melanie Daniels), Rod Taylor (Mitch Brenner), Jessica Tandy (Lydia Brenner), Suzanne Pleshette (Annie Hayworth), Veronika Cartwright (Cathy Brenner).
• Wealthy playgirl Melanie Daniels goes to the coastal village of Bodega Bay in pursuit of a man who has piqued her interest. After her arrival, thousands of birds attack the town for no apparent reason.

Marnie   **1964**
Screenplay Jay Presson Allen, based on a novel by Winston Graham. **Cinematography** Robert Burks. **Production** Universal, Geoffrey Stanley Inc. **Running time** 2h. With Tippi Hedren (Marnie Edgar), Sean Connery (Mark Rutland), Diane Baker (Lil), Louise Latham (Bernice Edgar), Martin Gabel (Sidney Strutt), Alan

Napier (Mr Rutland), Bruce Dern (Sailor).
• A rich man marries a compulsive thief who has tried to rob him and discovers on their wedding night that she is frigid as well. He then sets out to solve the mystery of the childhood trauma that caused her neurosis.

Torn Curtain   **1966**
Screenplay Brian Moore. **Cinematography** John F. Warren. **Production** Universal. **Running time** 2h 08. With Paul Newman (Michael Anderson), Julie Andrews (Sarah Sherman), Lila Kedrova (Countess Kuchinska), Wolfgang Kieling (Herrmann Gromek), Hansjoerg Felmy (Heinrich Gerhardt).
• To steal the secret of a Soviet antimissile missile, an American scientist pretends to defect to East Germany, but his fiancée decides to follow him.

Topaz   **1969**
Screenplay Samuel Taylor, based on a novel by Leon Uris. **Cinematography** Jack Hildyard. **Production** Universal. **Running time** 2h 05. With Frederick Stafford (André Devereaux), John Forsythe (Michael Nordstrom), Dany Robin (Nicole Devereaux), John Verson (Rico Parra), Karin Dor (Juanita De Cordoba), Michel Piccoli (Jacques Granville), Philippe Noiret (Henri Jarre), Claude Jade (Michèle Picard), Michel Subor (François Picard).
• A French spy is enlisted by the CIA for a dangerous mission in Cuba during the build-up to the 1962 missile crisis.

Frenzy   **1972**
Screenplay Anthony Schaffer, based on a novel by Arthur La Bern (Goodbye Piccadilly, Farewell Leicester Square). **Cinematography** Gil Taylor. **Production** Universal. **Running time** 1h 51. With Jon Finch (Richard Blaney), Barry Foster

(Robert Rusk), Barbara Leigh-Hunt (Brenda Blaney), Anna Massey (Babs Milligan), Alec McCowen (Chief Inspector Oxford), Vivien Merchant (Mrs Oxford), Billie Whitelaw (Hetty Porter).
• Richard Blaney is pursued by the police for the murder of his ex-wife, the latest victim of the Necktie Killer who is terrorizing London.

Family Plot   **1976**
Screenplay Ernest Lehman, based on a novel by Victor Canning (The Rainbird Pattern). **Cinematography** Leonard South. **Production** Universal. **Running time** 2h. With Karen Black (Fran), Bruce Dern (George Lumley), Barbara Harris (Blanche Tyler), William Devane (Arthur Adamson), Ed Lauter (Joseph Maloney), Cathleen Nesbitt (Julia Rainbird), Katherine Helmond (Mrs Maloney).
• Blanche and George, two con artists, try to find Edward Shoebridge, the long-lost nephew of the wealthy Julia Rainbird. But Edward, now a master criminal, doesn't want to be found.

Selected Bibliography

Raymond Bellour,
Analysis of film,
Indiana University Press,
Bloomington, 2001.

Peter Conrad,
The Hitchcock Murders,
Faber & Faber, London, 2000.

Bill Krohn,
Hitchcock at Work,
Phaidon Press, London, 2003.

Patrick McGilligan,
Alfred Hitchcock: A Life in Darkness and Light,
Regan Books, 2003.

Ken Mogg,
The Alfred Hitchcock Story,
Titan Books, London, 1999.

Jane E. Sloan,
Alfred Hitchcock:
A Guide to References and Resources,
G. K. Hall, Boston, 1983.

Donald Spoto,
The Dark Side of Genius: The Life of Alfred Hitchcock,
Da Capo Press, Cambridge, MA, 1999.

John Russell Taylor,
Hitch: The Life and Work of Alfred Hitchcock,
Faber & Faber, London, 1978.

François Truffaut,
Hitchcock/Truffaut,
Simon & Schuster, New York, 1986.

Robin Wood,
Hitchcock's Films Revisited,
Columbia University Press, New York, 1989.

Slavoj Žižek (ed.),
Everything You Wanted to Know About Lacan... but Were Afraid to Ask Hitchcock,
Verso Books, New York, 1988.

Notes

1. This was not a secret in 1948, as we can see from the remark by Georges Auriol: 'Why don't you ask your compatriot Liam O'Flaherty to write you a rather violent, rather savage film … Who knows? Perhaps a new James Joyce needs your collaboration. May St Patrick and St Brigid bring you together with that man!' (*La Revue du cinéma*, July 1948).

2. *Irish America Magazine*, 1998.

3. The exchanges between Hitchcock and Truffaut quoted throughout the book are all to be found in François Truffaut, *Hitchcock/Truffaut*, Simon and Schuster, New York, 1986.

4. Donald Spoto, *The Dark Side of Genius*, Little, Brown, New York, 1983, p.398.

5. Patrick McGilligan, *Alfred Hitchcock: A Life in Darkness and Light*, Regan Books, 2003.

6. Famous Players-Lasky was started in 1916 by the merger of Famous Players, founded in 1912 by Adolph Zukor, and the Jesse L. Lasky Feature Play Company. After the company was created, it absorbed Paramount Pictures Corporation, which was then its distribution company. Famous Players-Lasky subsequently became Paramount Pictures.

7. Graham Cutts, director of several films including *The Rat* (1925 with Ivor Novello), founded Gainsborough Pictures with Michael Balcon in 1924.

8. At this time UFA (Universum Film Aktien Gesellschaft) was the biggest German studio.

9. John Russell Taylor, *Hitch: The Life and Work of Alfred Hitchcock*, Faber & Faber, London, 1978.

10. Stephen Barr, *English Hitchcock*, Cameron & Hollis, 1999.

11. Hitchcock is to cinema what Velazquez was to painting, according to Pascal Bonitzer (*Le Champ aveugle*, Cahiers du cinéma, 1982). In *Las Meninas*, to display the deep structure of monocular perspective in painting, Velazquez used a mirror to reflect the king, who was outside the image, making him the privileged spectator of the painting.

12. The fact that – as is often the case in great English houses – there is a second stairway that is never shown (the backstairs, used by the servants) sometimes renders the movements of the characters incomprehensible.

13. David Bordwell and Kristin Thompson (in *Film Art: An Introduction*, McGraw-Hill, New York, 2003) cite Hitchcock as an example of what they call the 'hierarchy of knowledge' in classical cinema.

14. Hitchcock experienced the 'anxiety of influence', as the literary critic Harold Bloom named it (in *The Anxiety of Influence: A Theory of Poetry*, Oxford University Press, Oxford, 1973). To overcome the anxiety provoked by his precursor, the artist identifies with the precursor's precursor, thereby transforming his adversary into an inoffensive 'latecomer'.

15. The German filmmaker Fritz Lang started his career before Hitchcock, but after DeMille.

16. John Grierson, *Grierson on Documentary*, Praeger, 1966. An English left-wing critic, Grierson was the leader of the documentary movement that had such a great influence on English cinema after Hitchcock's departure. The prologues of Hitchcock's silent films that were filmed in a documentary style influenced the first documentaries of Grierson, who wrote, in his mixed review of *Murder!*, 'It still must be said that Hitchcock is the only English director who knows how to show the English poor in a halfway believable manner.'

17. Cf. David Bordwell, *Hitchcock: The Murderous Gaze*, Harvard University Press, Cambridge, MA, 1982.

18. Éric Rohmer and Claude Chabrol, *Hitchcock*, Éditions Universitaires, Paris, 1957.

19. For example, *Suspicion* (see Pascal Kané, *Cahiers du cinéma*, no. 228, March–April 1971).

20. A tangible sign of their sibling rivalry: the use of initials, in imitation of the DeMillian 'B'. As Peter Conrad has remarked (*The Hitchcock Murders*, Faber & Faber, London, 2000), Hitchcock's signature always included a 'J' (for Joseph). But Selznick's 'O' was meaningless: 'I had an uncle I didn't care for who was also named David Selznick, which is why, to avoid our being confused, I decided to add an initial to my name' (*Memo from David O. Selznick*, Modern Library, New York, 2000). Cf. the scene in *North by Northwest*: Eve: 'Roger O. Thornhill. What does the O stand for?' Thornhill: 'Nothing.'

21. Dilys Powell, the critic for the *Sunday Times* of London, wrote: 'this film is worth fifty Rebeccas.'

22. This theme was discovered and poorly used by Lesley Brill (*The Hitchcock Romance: Love and Irony in Hitchcock's Films*, Princeton University Press, Princeton, 1988).

23. Persephone appears in *The Pleasure Garden, The Lodger, Champagne, Blackmail, Sabotage* and *Jamaica Inn*, where the archetype takes on unmistakably sadomasochistic resonances.

24. *New Republic*, 14 February 1944, reprinted in *Farber on Film*, New American Library, New York, 2009, p.144.

25. See Robin Wood, *Hitchcock's Film Revisted*, Columbia University Press, New York, 1989.

26. Beginning with Jacques Rivette in 'Under Capricorn d'Alfred Hitchcock', *La Gazette du cinéma*, no.4, October 1950.

27. John Russell Taylor, Hitch: *The Life and Work of Alfred Hitchcock*, Faber & Faber, London, 1978.

28. André Bazin, *Le Cinéma de la cruauté*, Flammarion, Paris, 1975 (2nd edn 1987).

29. The impassive performance of Sessue Hayakawa in *The Cheat* had an enormous impact on cinema. It may even have inspired Hitchcock's idea of 'negative acting' (cf. Pascal Bonitzer, *Le Champ aveugle*).

Notes

30. This was the scene that Alexandre Astruc had in mind when he wrote in the first issue of *Cahiers du cinéma*: 'Like Maurice Scherer [Eric Rohmer], I would give all of *Stromboli* for that one shot in *Under Capricorn* where a woman's face is suddenly more vast than the sea' ('Au-dessous du volcan', *Cahiers du cinéma*, no.1, April 1951).

31. Which was political in the play. Paul Anthelme (a.k.a. Paul Bourde) had written a book under the pen name Paul Delion with the aim of discrediting the leaders of the Paris Commune, in which he said, 'Men, some from conviction, others from ambition, go around spreading socialist and egalitarian ideas, [but these ideas] have an effect exactly contrary to their stated aim.' *Nos deux consciences* illustrates the same idea.

32. Louis Skorecki, *Les Violons ont toujours raison*, PUF, Paris, 2000.

33. The religion in which the birth of the cosmos is a fall is Gnosticism, in which Creation was the work of the Demiurge, the inept creator of a material cosmos in which fragments of divinity were scattered and imprisoned when they fell. This confirms Douchet's argument that Hitchcock's metaphysics has as least as much to do with Gnosticism as it does with Catholicism (see Jean Douchet, *Hitchcock*, L'Herne, Paris, 1967; revised edition published by Cahiers du cinéma in the 'Petite bibliotheque des Cahiers du cinema' series, 1999). It is no accident that Douchet's book has the same title as that of Chabrol and Rohmer, because he is proposing a radical – even heretical – revision of their thesis that Hitchcock is a Catholic artist. According to the literary theorist Harold Bloom, 'Gnosticism is the religion of all artists, for whom the precursor plays the role of the Demiurge, and his precursor, that of the true God.'

34. In the first episode of the series, the numbers on the licence plate of a car add up to 13, the number of all new beginnings, including Hitchcock's own. He was born on August 13, and his first, unfinished film was called *Number 13*.

35. Jean Douchet, *Hitchcock*, Cahiers du cinéma, Paris, 1999 (first published 1967).

36. Ian Cameron, 'Hitchcock and the Mechanisms of Suspense', *Movie*, no. 3, October 1962.

37. 'That cry that signals her defeat is the first manifestation of her liberty and her ultimate salvation' (Éric Rohmer and Claude Chabrol, *Hitchcock*).

38. Bill Krohn, *Hitchcock au travail*, Cahiers du cinéma, Paris, 1999.

39. An ironic miracle is recounted in 'The Horseplayer' (1961), an episode of *Alfred Hitchcock Presents* directed by Hitchcock on the subject of the efficacy of prayer.

40. Ken Mogg, *The Alfred Hitchcock Story*, Titan Books, London, 1999.

41. *Male and Female* (1919) and the astonishing *The Road to Yesterday* (1925), which starts off with a honeymoon as glacial as the one in *Marnie*.

42. *Liliom* (1934), Lang's only French film, is also the story of a fatal repetition: a hoodlum who kills himself comes back to life for a single day to do a good deed, but he fails.

43. *In The Thousand Eyes of Dr. Mabuse* (1961), Mabuse uses multiple TV screens to spy on the other characters. When TV finally puts in its first appearance in a Hitchcock film five years later, in *Torn Curtain*, it appears in the form of multiple screens, and it is German television at that.

44. *North by Northwest* was written by Ernest Lehman, who went on to script the movie version of *West Side Story*, the hit play Roger is supposed to see with his mother before he's kidnapped by Russian spies who think he's the red herring, George Kaplan. Bernard Herrmann's thrilling score actually appropriates the 6/8 time signature and descending thirds of *West Side Story*'s 'America' number in the Fandango that is the film's main theme.

45. Dennis Perry, *Hitchcock and Poe: The Legacy of Delight and Terror*, Scarecrow Press, Lanham, MD, 2003. In a short article on *The Birds* in *Cahiers du cinéma* Jean-Louis Comolli detects another echo in the shot of the gulls descending to attack the town: 'The scattering of the gulls imitates the scythe's movement. Calm, waiting, forgetfulness, immobility … cannot oppose their fragile inalterability to the pendulum, whose rigour enlarges the circle it makes around its centre.'

46. Sumiko Higahsi, *Cecil B. DeMille and American Culture: The Silent Era*, University of California Press, Berkeley, 1994.

47. Whom Hitchcock had wanted to play Cary Grant's adversary in *North by Northwest*.

48. He wrote her a letter expressing his regret and included a tape-recording for Prince Rainier of a joke 'not for all ears', which he knew Kelly would listen to before passing it on. The unusual method it described for capturing tapeworms was a ribald variant on the story of Winston Graham's novel about how society rids itself of a talented parasite – a beautiful girl who is a compulsive thief and sexually frigid – told from the tapeworm's point of view.

49. Murray Pomerance goes so far as to describe *Marnie* as a Southern rebel stealing the riches of the North in *An Eye for Hitchcock*, Rutgers University Press, Piscataway, NJ, 2004.

50. Wasserman was quite happy to produce thrillers in the Hitchcock manner by lesser filmmakers, such as *Charade* by Stanley Donen (1963) and *Cape Fear* by J. Lee Thompson (1962).

51. Joseph McBride, 'Alfred Hitchcock's *Mary Rose*: An Old Master's Unheard *Cri du Cœur*', *Cinéaste*, 26(2), 2001.

52. Hitchcock's situation is ambiguous. For Rohmer and Chabrol (*Hitchcock*) he is 'the greatest inventor of forms in the history of cinema'; for Douchet and Skorecki he is, from the 1950s on, the inventor of a 'post-cinema' that bears witness to a sad devolution. ('Hitchcock in *Family Plot* portrays the degeneration of cinema,' writes Douchet in his *Hitchcock*).

53. Bill Krohn, 'A Hitchcock Mystery', *The MacGuffin*, no. 27, December 2000. It was Ken Mogg, the editor of *The MacGuffin*, who found an article identifying the text read during the funeral of Joseph Maloney, keeper of the childhood secrets of Arthur Adamson. But where did the idea of making the deceased a Mormon come from? Hitchcock and screenwriter Ernest Lehman had a problem: for George (Bruce Dern) to be able to pick up Adamson's trail, he had to have grown up in a town whose inhabitants (a) never left the spot where they were born and (b) maintained impeccable genealogical archives. Perhaps Dern, who comes from Utah, suggested the idea, which also seems to have caused an Old Testament-style beard to sprout on Maloney's face.

Sources

Courtesy of Academy of Motion Pictures of Arts and Science: p. 39 (bottom), 43, 49 (bottom), 66–7, 71, 74, 76, 94 (2nd col. bottom), 98 (1st col. bottom).
BFI Collection: p. 7, 10, 96 (2nd col. top).
Collection BIFI: p. 96 (2nd col. centre and bottom; 3rd col. top), 97 (1st col. top and centre).
Collection Cahiers du cinéma: cover, inside front cover, p. 2–3, 6, 8, 9 (bottom), 11, 14–5, 16–7, 18–9, 27, 28, 29, 30–1, 33, 34, 36–7, 39 (bottom), 40–1, 44–5, 47, 48, 50–1, 52–3, 54–5, 57, 58, 59, 60, 63, 64, 68 (bottom), 70, 73 (bottom), 77, 79 (top and bottom), 80, 81, 88, 89, 90–1, 92, 93, 94 (1st col.; 2nd col. top; 3rd col.), 95 (1st col.; 2nd col.; 3rd col. top and bottom), 96 (3rd col. centre and bottom; 4th col. top), 97 (3rd col. top and bottom; 4th col. centre and bottom), 98 (1st col. top; 2nd col. top and centre; 3rd col. top, centre and bottom; 4th col. top), 99 (1st col. top and bottom; 2nd col. centre and bottom; 4th col. centre), 100 (1st col. bottom; 2nd col. top and bottom; 3rd col.), inside back cover.
Collection Cahiers du cinéma / Dominique Rabourdin: p. 56, 99 (1st col. centre).
Collection CAT'S: p. 72 (left), 72–3.
Collection Cinémathèque française: p. 12–3, 20, 21, 22 (top), 22–3, 24–5, 26–7, 32, 39 (top), 46, 96 (1st col bottom; 4th col. centre), 97 (1st col. bottom; 2nd col. top, centre and bottom; 4th col. bottom), 98 (1st col. centre; 2nd col. bottom).
Collection François Rivière: p. 94 (4th col.).
Collection Gilles Gressard: p. 61, 64, 69 (right), 83 (top), 99 (3rd col. top and centre), 100 (1st col. centre).
Collection Magnum: p. 95 (4th col.).
Collection TCD: 83 (bottom), 86–7.
Screen grabs: p. 9 (top), 49 (top), 62, 68 (top), 69 (left), 75 (top to bottom), 82 (top to bottom), 84 (top to bottom), 96 (1st col. top and centre; 4th col. bottom), 98 (4th col. centre and bottom), 99 (3rd col. bottom; 4th col. top and bottom), 100 (1st col. top; 2nd col. centre).

Credits

© 20th Century Fox Film Corporation: p. 40–1, 98 (3rd col. top).
© Alfred Hitchcock's Estate: p. 7, 95 (3rd col. top and bottom).
© BIP: inside back cover, inside front cover, 11, 14–5, 18–9, 20, 21, 22 (top), 16–7, 96 (2nd col. bottom; 3rd col. top, centre and bottom; 4th col. top, centre and bottom), 97 (1st col. top, centre and bottom).
© David O'Selznick: p. 98 (4th col. top).
© Disney Pictures: p. 34, 98 (1st col. top).
© Emelka GBA: p. 6, 8, 9, 96 (1st col. top).
© Gainsborough: p. 9 (bottom), 10, 12–3, 96 (1st col. centre and bottom; 2nd col. top and centre).
© Gaumont British Pictures: p. 24–5, 26, 28, 29, p. 30–1, 32, 33, 94 (1st col.), 97 (2nd col. centre and bottom; 3rd col. top and bottom; 4th col. top, centre and bottom).
© MGM / United Artists: p. 39 (top), 98 (1st col. centre).
© Paramount: p. 27.
© Philippe Halsman / Magnum: p. 95 (4th col.).
© Tom Arnold Productions: p. 22–3, 97 (2nd col. top).
© Universal City Studios: p. 95 (2nd col.), 99 (3rd col. centre), 100 (2nd col. centre).
© Universal Pictures: cover, p. 2–3, 4–5, 39 (bottom), 46, 50–1, 58, 59, 60, 61, 63, 65, 66–7, 68 (top), 69 (both), 70, 72 (left), 72–3, 73, 79 (top to bottom), 80, 81, 82, 83 (top to bottom), 84, 85–6, 88, 89, 90–1, 92, 93, 98 (2nd col. centre and bottom; 4th col. centre), 99 (2nd col. bottom; 3rd col. top, centre and bottom), 100 (1st col. top, centre and bottom; 2nd col. top and bottom), 100 (3rd col.).
© Universal TV: p. 62.
© Warner Bros Ent. Inc: p. 36–7, 43, 44–5, 47, 48, 49 (top to bottom), 52–3, 54–5, 56, 57, 64, 68 (bottom), 71, 74, 75, 76, 77, 98 (2nd col. top; 3rd col. centre and bottom; 4th col. bottom), 99 (1st col. top and bottom; 2nd col. top and centre; 4th col. top and bottom).
© Warner Bros Pictures: p. 94 (2nd col. bottom; 3rd col.).

Cover: Alfred Hitchcock in 1963.
Inside front cover: Alfred Hitchcock in *Blackmail* (1929).
Inside back cover: Henry Kendall, Joan Barry and Betty Amann in *Rich and Strange* (1932).

Acknowledgements

Ken Mogg, Émilie Saada, Patrick McGilligan, Lillian and Harold Michelson, Joe Kaufman, Samuel Brean, Murray Pomerance, Dan Sallitt, Barbara Hall, Mike Thomas, Erwan Higuinen, Michael and Carole Wilson, Brent Kite, Andy Rector, Ronnie Scheib, Alan David Vertrees, Will Schmenner, Sarah Street, Joe Dante, Véronique Isoardi-Morales, Joseph McBride, Natasha Banon, Bernard Eisenschitz.

Cahiers du cinéma Sarl
65, rue Montmartre
75002 Paris

www.cahiersducinema.com

Revised English Edition © 2010 Cahiers du cinéma Sarl
First published in French as *Alfred Hitchcock* © 2007 Cahiers du cinéma Sarl

ISBN 978 2 8664 2571 5

A CIP catalogue record of this book is available from the British Library.

Series conceived by Claudine Paquot
Designed by Werner Jeker/Les Ateliers du Nord
Printed in China